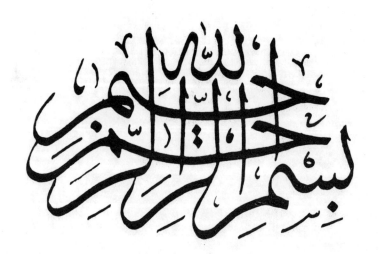

SHAMAIL-E-TIRMIZI

by

Imam Abu Isa Tirmizi

With Notes From

Shaikh Al-Hadith Maulana Muhammad Zakaria
&
Shaikh Al-Hadith Mufti Ahmed E. Bemat

Translated by

Prof. Murtaza Hussain F. Qurashi

KITAB BHAVAN
NEW DELHI-110002

Kitab Bhavan
Publishers, Distributors, Exporters & Importers
1784, Kalan Mahal, Darya Ganj
New Delhi - 1100 02 (India)

Phone   :   (91-11) 23277392/93, 23274686, 30906494
website :   www.kitabbhavan.com
Email   :   nasri@vsnl.com
Fax   :   (91-11) 23263383

First Edition   1997
IInd Reprinted 2006

ISBN   : 81-7151-232-1
Code No. : S00330

Published in India by :
Nusrat Ali Nasri for Kitab Bhavan
1784, Kalan Mahal, Darya Ganj
New Delhi - 1100 02 [India]

Printed in India at :
Nice Printing Press
Khureji Khas, Delhi-110051

CONTENTS

THE PHYSICAL CHARACTER OF THE HOLY PROPHET (S.A.W.)

FOREWORD

The personality and character of the Prophet Muhammad (p.b.u.h.) constituted a model example for the Muslims. His life represents not only the practical demonstration as to how we should practise the teachings of the Qur'an but also constitutes the perennial source of guidance and inspiration. Muslim scholars have taken pains to preserve all relevant material about the life and career of the Prophet of Islam. Starting with the details about his personal features and habits upto his life style and conduct in dealing with others have been painstakingly preserved by the early doctors of Hadith and vouchsafed to the posterity.

Imam Tirmizi's well-known collection on the *Shamail* [Habits and Traits of the Prophet (p.b.u.h.)] has been one of the basic and popular sources on the subject. It has been translated into several languages of the world including English. The illustrious author and compiler of the book, Imam Abu Isa Tirmizi has collected original material reported on the authority of the Companions of the Holy Prophet (p.b.u.h.) himself. It has always been considered to be one of the primary sources on the personality and character of the Prophet (p.b.u.h.) of Islam and has always served as a textbook and an enrichment material for Muslim students.

We feel pleasure in bringing out this edition of the *Shamail* in English language. The present English translation is based on Urdu version prepared along with minor explanatory notes by late Maulana Muhammad Zakariya. We pray Almighty Allah to give reward to all those respectable scholars who were instrumental in making this material available to us.

—**Dr. Mahmood A. Ghazi**

I

IN THE NAME OF ALLAH
(THE COMPASSIONATE, THE MERCIFUL, PRAISE BE TO ALLAH AND PEACE BE ON HIS CHOSEN SLAVES)!

Sheikh Hafiz Abu Isa Muhammad Ibn Isa Tirmizi says :

CHAPTER :-- The traditional Reports regarding the Holy Prophet's (*sallallaho alaihe wa sallam!*) holy physiognomy are as follows :--

NOTE :-- It is beyond human power to draw a pen-picture of the Holy Prophet's (*sallallaho alaihe wa sallam!*) physiognomy; It is not within the capacity of anyone to describe light incarnate. However, the noble Companions (*razi Allaho anhum!*), as per their light and capacity, have tried to describe his features to give us glimpse of him and satisfy us thereby.

Allamah Qurtabi (mercy be on him!) says that the whole of the Holy Prophet's (*sallallaho alaihe wa sallam!*) handsomeness had not been manifested as otherwise the people would not have been able to cast a glance at him.

A Persian poet has remarked truly that all the handsomeness that was possessed by different prophets and apostles had found consummate expression in the Last Holy Prophet (*sallallaho alaihe wa sallam!*).

9

While Prophet Joseph's handsomeness had no veil over it there was a veil over the Holy Prophet's (*sallallaho alaihe wa sallam!*) elegance.

It is indeed the noble Companions' (*razi Allaho anhum!*) great obligation over the *ummah* that they not only recorded and transmitted the Holy Prophet's (*sallallaho alaihe wa sallam!*) sciences but they also made an effort to describe his physical features and succeeded in this effort (to an appreciable extent).

Hazrat Br'a ibn 'Azib (*razi Allaho anho!*) says that he never saw any person more handsome than the Holy Prophet (*sallallaho alaihe wa sallam!*).

In another tradition (*riwayat*) says Hazrat Ali (*razi Allaho anho!*) that an eulogist of the Holy Prophet (*sallallaho alaihe wa sallam!*) would say that he never saw anyone more handsome either prior to him or subsequently.

Hazrat Hind (*razi Allaho anho!*) says that the Holy Prophet's (*sallallaho alaihe wa sallam!*) auspicious face shone like the full moon.

Hazrat Jabir (*razi Allaho anho!*) reports that once, during a moonlit night, "I was looking at the Holy Prophet (*sallallaho alaihe wa sallam!*) as well as at the moon, but, according to my opinion, the Holy Prophet (*sallallaho alaihe wa sallam!*) was more beautiful than the moon".

Hazrat Abu Huraira (*razi Allaho anho!*) reports that the Holy Prophet (*sallallaho alaihe wa sallam!*) was so white that it seemed as if he had been made out of silver.

Hadith 1 :-- Hazrat Anas (*razi Allaho anho!*) used to say that the Holy Prophet (*sallallaho alaihe wa sallam!*) was neither very tall nor very short (and his complexion was neither absolutely white like lime nor sallow).

The Holy Prophet's (*sallallaho alaihe wa sallam!*) auspicious hair were neither absolutely straight nor absolutely curly (like those of the negroes). The Holy Lord bestowed prophethood upon him when he was forty years of age.

Note regarding complexion - He was not white. He was not as white as lime. Similarly his complexion was not wheaten. The meaning is that his whiteness had a touch of redness.

Allamah Ibrahim Baijori (mercy be upon him!) writes in his *Mawahib* (p.7) that in this world this colour looks very graceful that there may be redness with whiteness and in the Hereafter there may be paleness with whiteness. So the Holy Prophet's (*sallallaho alaihe wa sallam!*) white complexion had a touch of redness and there was a luster in it.

Note 1:- Hence the *Imams* have stated that "if someone says that the Holy Prophet's (*sallallaho alaihe wa sallam!*) complexion was black, we will issue a *fatwa* of infidelity (*Kufr*) for him because he insulted and disparaged the Holy Prophet (*sallallaho alaihe wa sallam!*), and the insulting and disparaging of a prophet amounts to infidelity; and since it is a falsification of a number of continuous (*mutawatir*) hadiths by which his being white in complexion is proved, we shall call the man who denies continuous hadiths an infidel" (*Mawahib* p.8)

11

Note 2:- It is established from the aforementioned hadith that the Holy Prophet's (*sallallaho alaihe wa sallam!*) height was medium. Another tradition has it that whenever he was in the midst of a group of people, he (*sallallaho alaihe wa sallam!*) used to look taller than others. The implication of this hadith is that it was the Holy Prophet's (*sallallaho alaihe wa sallam!*) miracle that he used to look taller than others; even as he was greater than others in knowledge and morals, he used to appear taller than others in physical stature.

Note 3:- It appears from the said hadith that his auspicious age was sixty years whereas in famous hadiths it is sixty-three years. So why this divergence in hadiths?

Answer 1:- Prophethood was bestowed at the age of 40 years and apostleship 3 years later. The said 3 years were omitted in the statement through oversight.

Answer 2:- Usually exact age is mentioned in conversation and fractions are omitted and hence it was mentioned in decades only.

Necessary Explanation:- If a man has Rs.550/- and he is asked how much money he has, he usually says that he has five hundred rupees.

When a man goes on a journey and turns after 32 or 33 days, he usually says that he spent a month in the journey.

The man who returns after 45 days from a Tabligh journey, he usually says that he completed a *chilla* (40 days). There is no divergence regarding months; the tens were mentioned and the digits were omitted.

Hadith 2:- Hazrat Ali (*razi Allaho anho!*) says that the Holy Prophet (*sallallaho alaihe wa sallam!*) was neither tall nor short. His auspicious palms and both the feet were fleshy. The auspicious head was large; the joint-bones were also large. From the chest to the navel there was a thin line of hair. When he walked, it appeared as if he was descending from a higher place.

Hazrat Ali (*razi Allaho anho!*) also reports that he did not see a more handsome face, either formerly or subsequently, than that of the Holy Prophet (*sallallaho alaihe wa sallam!*).

Note:- The description given in the aforesaid hadiths is factual. Besides the spiritual perfection, the Holy Prophet (*sallallaho alaihe wa sallam!*) was pearless in external physical features as well. Hence Allamah Manavi (mercy be on him!), has stated that it is necessary for every Muslim to cherish the belief that no other human being could ever be like the Holy Prophet (*sallallaho alaihe wa sallam!*); he was incomparable among the created beings.

It appears from reading books of biography, history and hadith that neither anyone had such face and features as those of the Holy Prophet (*sallallaho alaihe wa sallam!*) nor would ever be given such face and features.

From Hazrat Ayesha Siddiqa (*razi Allaho anha!*) have been recorded two couplets which mean: 'Had Zulaikha's female friends who had cut their hands on having a glimpse of Joseph (peace be on him!) seen the Holy Prophet (*sallallaho alaihe wa sallam!*) they would have cut their hearts instead'.

It is quite true. If you want to see a sample of the noble Companions' and lady-Companions' deep love for the Holy Prophet (*sallallaho alaihe wa sallam!*), I would request you to read Shaikh al-Hadith Maulana Zakariya Sahib's Hikayat-e-Sahaba (The Stories of the Companions).

Hadith 3:- It is reported from Hazrat Ibrahim ibn Muhammad (mercy be on him!), Hazrat Ali's (razi Allah anho!) grandson, that whenever Hazrat Ali described the Holy Prophet (*sallallaho alaihe wa sallam!*), he always used to say that the Holy Prophet (*sallallaho alaihe wa sallam!*) was neither very tall nor very short but had a body like that of the medium-sized people. His hair were neither quite straight nor quite curly, but besides being straight were somewhat wavy. The body was not thick; similarly, the face was not round but was oval.

The Holy Prophet's (*sallallaho alaihe wa sallam!*) complexion was fair with a touch of redness. The eyes were very black and the hair of the eye-brows were long. The bones of the joints in the body were thick (wrist, elbow, knee). The space between the shoulders was fleshy. The holy body was not hairy (i.e., excepting the particular parts of the body, there were no hair all over the body); however, there was a line of hair from the chest to the navel. The auspicious hands and feet were fleshy. When the Holy Prophet (*sallallaho alaihe wa sallam!*) walked, he used to step forward firmly; it appeared as if he was walking towards a low one. When he paid attention to anyone, he did so with all his body (i.e... like proud people, he did not pay attention carelessly or by merely turning the eyes, but would wheel around his whole auspicious body and turn his lustrous face to pay attention). Between his shoulders was the Seal of Prophethood. The office of prophethood ended with him. He was more magnanimous than all the creatures and more truthful in speaking than all and more softhearted than all. He belonged to the noblest family.

Necessary Explanation:- As regards heart, tongue, disposition, family and personal and familial characteristics, the Holy Prophet (*sallallaho alaihe wa sallam!*) was superior to all. Anyone who looked at him casually used to be overawed. External and internal good qualities and virtues had so combined in him that a casual look at him filled a stranger's heart with terror, but those who came in close contact with him used to fall in love with him due to his loving disposition and excellent morals. In fact a person who came in close contact with him used to make him the most beloved person. One who would describe his face and features could say only this much that "I never saw, either before or after having seen the Holy Prophet (*sallallaho alaihe wa sallam!*) any person possessing such external and internal beauties".

Hadith 4:- The Holy Prophet's (*sallallaho alaihe wa sallam!*) grandson, Hazrat Hasan (*razi Allaho anho!*) was only seven years of age at the Holy Prophet (*sallallaho alaihe wa sallam!*) demise. He also says: "I inquired from my maternal-uncle Hind ibn Abi Halah, about the Holy Prophet's (*sallallaho alaihe wa sallam!*) face and figure, for he often used to describe him in great detail. I too wished that he should describe his charming qualities before me so that I make his description a proof and an argument for myself and, having fixed those excellent qualities in my mind, I try, as far as possible, to put them into practice. So he (Hind ibn Abi Halah) said:-

15

'The Holy Prophet (*sallallaho alaihe wa sallam!*) was great by virtue of his own personality and was also great in the eyes of others. His face shone like the full moon. He was taller in stature than a man of average height but shorter than a very tall man. The auspicious head was moderately large: though it was large, it looked appropriately handsome; it was not so large as to mar the handsomeness of the face and the figure. The auspicious hair were somewhat wavy (i.e., were not absolutely straight). He did not care to part the hair; if the hair could be parted easily, well and good, otherwise he did not pay special attention to doing so. In this matter he acted according to time and circumstances: if, after applying oil, a comb was at hand, he would part the hair and if a comb was not readily available, he would part the hair when he could lay his hands on a comb.

'When the Holy Prophet's (*sallallaho alaihe wa sallam!*) hair were long, they reached a little farther than his ear-lobes. His complexion was lustrous and the auspicious forehead was wide. The eye-brows were thin and arched; they were also separate, not joined. Between them was a vein that used to swell up whenever he felt angry. His auspicious nose looked high, having a shine and lustre on it. At first an onlooker would think him to be large-nosed but when one looked at him minutely one felt that the nose appeared high due to lustre and was not actually large.

The auspicious beard was luxuriant. The pupils of the eye were very black. The auspicious cheeks were even (not sunken); they were fleshy but not flabby and flaccid.

His holiness's auspicious mouth was moderately broad (and not narrow whereby one looks ungraceful);

16

the teeth were small and shining (and not large). There was also some distance between the front teeth; they were not very close to each other. There was a thin line of hair from the chest to the navel.

The neck was thin and good-looking, like that of a well-chiselled iron, and in complexion, it was fair and attractive like silver. All his limbs were moderately muscular; the body was robust. The stomach and the auspicious chest were even (i.e., there was no potbelly which would inconvenience walking). But the chest was wide and there was somewhat greater distance between the two shoulders. The bones of the joints were big and strong (which is a sign of strength). When he put off his clothes, the body looked sheeny and lustrous. (Those parts of the body that remained bare were as sheeny and bright as those that were covered by clothes). There was a line of hair between the chest and the stomach; except this, both the chest and the stomach were free from hair but there were hair on both the arms, shoulders and the upper part of the chest. His wrists were long and palms wide; both the feet were fleshy and plump. The fingers of the hands and the feet were long symmetrically; the soles were deep and the feet even. Due to the smoothness of the feet, water did not stay on them but flowed off immediately. When he walked he used to step forth firmly. He walked with a slight forward bent, putting his feet on the ground lightly and not heavily. He used to walk with vigorous strides and would not take short steps. When he walked it appeared as if he was walking downhill.

When the Holy Prophet (*sallallaho alaihe wa sallam!*) paid attention, he did so with his entire body. His auspicious eyes remained down-cast; they were directed mostly towards the earth rather than towards the sky. It is stated in a tradition of the *Abu Da'ud Sharif* that he used to look towards the sky frequently. But there is no divergence between the two hadiths. While awaiting divine revelation (*wahy*), he often used to look skyward, otherwise normally he would look only towards the earth.

It was his noble habit usually to see through the corners of his eyes; i.e., due to extreme bashfulness and modestly, he did not gaze at anyone.

While walking, he used to keep the Companions ahead of himself and he remained behind them; and whomsoever he met in the way, he used to be the first to greet.

Note:- For the Holy Prophet (*sallallaho alaihe wa sallam!*) gait has been used the word *"yatkaf'a"* which has been translated in three ways: (1) He used to walk briskly; (2) he used to walk bending his neck forward; and (3) he used to take vigorous steps. All the three translations are correct. The Holy Prophet (*sallallaho alaihe wa sallam!*), bending his neck forward out of humility, used to walk vigorously and did not protrude his chest like the proud people while walking or did not drag along like women, and he would never glance at the people's houses.

Necessary Explanation:- While walking, the brave always lift their feet properly; the Holy Prophet (*sallallaho alaihe wa sallam!*) who used to value every second and minute would always walk very briskly; he did not while away his time like the present-day people, and would always bend his head down while walking. The chaste and the virtuous feel ashamed of looking at others' defects, and hence he used to walk with modesty, devouteness and humility.

18

Note 1: The Holy Prophet (*sallallaho alaihe wa sallam!*) while walking, used to remain behind others out of his innate humility. The practice of the haughty and the egotistical in the world is that they consider it a mark of honour, status and dignity to be in the forefront while walking with others. Hence the Companions have reported that he (*sallallaho alaihe wa sallam!*) used to walk behind others.

Note 2:- During journey, he would remain in the rear with the intention of helping those who needed help. If the goods of any Companion were left behind, he would pick them up and thus help his Companions.

Necessary Explanation:- (1) Allamah Baijori has stated that angels used to walk behind the Holy Prophet (*sallallaho alaihe wa sallam!*) and hence he would keep the Companions ahead and himself walk in the rear. (2). The Holy Prophet (*sallallaho alaihe wa sallam!*) was an affectionate teacher by keeping his disciples in the front he used to train them, teaching civil mores (*adab*) to those who lacked in them and pointing out shortcomings in those who had such shortcomings. And the last words of the hadith are that he used to precede others in saluting.

Necessary Explanation:- (i) Even if he came across small children, he used to salute them. (ii) Like the haughty and the proud he did not wait for the salutation of others; rather, he himself made haste in greeting others. (iii) Saluting is an act of sunnah; to answer it is indispensable (*wajib*), but here the recompense of the sunnah is greater than that of an indispensable act and hence he used to be prompt in saluting. (iv) The aforesaid acts were meant to be imparted to the *ummah*.

May Allah bestow upon us the grace to follow and practise them! Amen!

Hadith 5:- Hazrat Jabir (*razi Allaho anho!*) says: "Once, during a moonlit night, I was looking at the Holy Prophet (*sallallaho alaihe wa sallam!*). He was at that time wearing a red suit (a lungi and a shirt having red stripes). Sometimes I was glancing at the moon and sometime at him. At last I decided that the Holy Prophet (*sallallaho alaihe wa sallam!*) was more handsome, charming and lustrous than the moon".

Hadith 6: Hazrat Abu Huraira (*razi Allaho anho!*) says: "The Holy Prophet (*sallallaho alaihe wa sallam!*) was so fair, handsome and good looking that it seemed as if his body had been made of silver. His hair were somewhat curly.

Hadith 7:- Hazrat Abd Allah ibn Abbas (*razi Allaho anho!*) states that the Holy Prophet (*sallallaho alaihe wa sallam!*) frontal teeth were a little distant from each other; they were not very close. Whenever he spoke, a light was seen emitting from between his teeth.

Note:- Some ulema are of the opinion that it is a simile; it looked like light. But Allamah Manavi (mercy be on him!) writes that the said light used to emit from between the teeth.

His auspicious eyes, in looks, were like ours, but he used to see in darkness also even as we see in light.

Hazrat Ayesha (*razi Allaho anha!*) reports that the Holy Prophet (*sallallaho alaihe wa sallam!*) could sight things in darkness even as he saw them in light.

20

It is reported from Hazrat Abu Huraira (*razi Allaho anho!*) that the Holy Prophet (*sallallaho alaihe wa sallam!*) said: "Do you think that I see only from the front? By Allah! Your genuflections (*ruku'*) and your prostrations (*sajdah*) are not hidden from me. Undoubtedly I see you with my back also". It is related from Hazrat Anas (*razi Allaho anho!*) that the Holy Prophet (*sallallaho alaihe wa sallam!*) said: "O people! I am your imam. Don't look at me while performing genuflections and prostrations. I look with my back as well as from my front". Besides these, there are traditions related by other Companions too that the Holy Prophet (*sallallaho alaihe wa sallam!*) could see through his back also. The ulema have stated that he used to see through the same eyes and it was a prophetic miracle. Neither cloth nor any other thing could become a veil or an obstruction for him.

* * * * * * * *

21

II

THE DESCRIPTION OF "THE SEAL OF PROPHETHOOD"

Physical features, of the Holy Prophet (*sallallaho alaihe wa sallam!*) have been described in the preceding chapter. The Seal of Prophethood is a unique thing, a thing of great importance and significance; it is a miracle and an incontrovertible sign of prophethood, and hence I thought it deserved to be dealt with in a separate chapter.

The Seal of Prophethood was there on the Holy Prophet (*sallallaho alaihe wa sallam!*) body since his childhood – a tradition that has been reported in the *Fat-al-Bari* from Hazrat Ayesha (*razi Allaho anha!*) – and when the Holy Prophet (*sallallaho alaihe wa sallam!*) breathed his last and some Companions were not ready to believe that he was dead, Hazrat Asma (*razi Allaho anha!*) argued on the strength of the Seal of Prophethood that it was then no more extent, which meant and proved that the death had taken place.

Ibn Hibban has stated that "MUHAMMAD RASULALLAH" was written on the Seal of Prophethood, while certain other traditions say that "Antal Mansur" was inscribed on it. This inscription means: "Go wherever you like, you will be succoured". To prove the existence of this Seal of Prophethood, Imam Tirmizi has stated eight traditions out of which I am quoting below only five:-

Hadith 1:- Hazrat Sa'ib ibn Yazid (*razi Allaho anho!*) reports: "My maternal aunt took me to the Holy Prophet (*sallallaho alaihe wa sallam!*) and said 'My nephew is ill'. So he drew his auspicious hand affectionately over my head and invoked prosperity (*barka*) for me. Then he performed ablution (*wuzu*) and I drank the water that had remained from the ablution. Then I stood behind him and saw the Seal of Prophethood which was like a knot of curtain that is put on the bedstead".

Note:- The reason for drawing the hand over the head was affection and mercy; or there was some ailment and hence he passed his hand over Sa'ib's head so that with the blessing of the auspicious hand the disease was removed.

Hadith 2:- Hazrat Jabir (*razi Allaho anho!*) reports that he saw the Seal of Prophethood in the middle of the Holy Prophet's (*sallallaho alaihe wa sallam!*) shoulders; it was like a red-coloured tumour and as big as a pigeon's egg.

Note:-- As regards the size and colour of the Seal of Prophethood the traditions seem to be at variance, but, as a matter of fact, there is no variance, because there used to be fluctuation in the size and colour of the Seal of Prophethood. (*Khasa'is-e Kubra*, p.60).

The second thing is that the Companions who had seen it have compared it by way of guess and individual estimates always tend to differ. Hence differences in a description based on guesswork and surmise are of no importance.

Hadith 3:- Hazrat 'Ilba' ibn Ahmar says that 'Amr ibn Akhtab' (*razi Allaho anho!*) narrated this incident to

23

him:- "Once the Holy Prophet (*sallallaho alaihe wa sallam!*) asked me to massage his waist. I began to massage it. By chance my finger touched the Seal of Prophethood". When 'Llba' asked "Amr as to what this Seal of Prophethood was, he said: "It was a mass of hair".

This version seems to be contradictory to the aforesaid traditions but in fact there is no contradiction, for the Seal of Prophethood was like a lump of flesh in which there used to be fluctuations. There were wart-like moles around it and on them were hair. Hence some called it a mass of hair, some said it was a wart, some compared it to a knot and some described it as a pigeon's egg.

Hadith 4:- Hazrat Buraidh (*razi Allaho anho!*) reports that when the Holy Prophet (*sallallaho alaihe wa sallam!*) emigrated to Medina, Hazrat Salman Farsi (*razi Allaho anho!*) brought a tray full of fresh dates and offered it to him. He asked, "What is this"? Salman said: "it is sacrifice (*sadaqah*) for you and your Companions". He said: "we do not eat *sadaqah*". On the second day too Salman came with a tray of dates and said: "These dates are a gift". Then the Holy Prophet (*sallallaho alaihe wa sallam!*) and the Companions ate of those dates. Thereafter Salman saw the Seal of Prophethood and embraced Islam.

Note 1:- Allamah Baijori has pointed out that Hazrat Salman Farsi was one of the religious scholars of ancient times. His age was nearly 250 years; according to another statement, it was 350 years. He had read about the tokens of the last prophet in his own religious books which mentioned that the last prophet would decline sadaqah and accept gift (*hadyah*) and would have a seal of prophethood on his body. When Salman had tested

24

whether these three tokens were present or not and when he was satisfied, he became a Muslim. The information about these tokens was given to him by Christian monks also.

Note 2:- It was stated in the above hadith that the Holy Prophet (*sallallaho alaihe wa sallam!*) said ; "We do not eat sadaqah". So, who are meant by 'we'? Regarding this divergence of opinion certain ulema maintain that the pronoun 'we', which is first person plural, has been used for his own noble and honourable person, and some ulema say that by 'we' is meant the group of prophets, whereas other ulema assert that by this pronoun are meant the Holy Prophet (*sallallaho alaihe wa sallam!*), himself and his kith and kin for whom the partaking of sadaqah is prohibited (*haram*). The last reasoning is correct because the legal proposition (*mas'ala*) is also the same.

Note 3:- It is further stated that in the said hadith that the Holy Prophet (*sallallaho alaihe wa sallam!*) bought Hazrat Salman, who was a Jew's slave. In fact it was not buying, for the Holy Prophet (*sallallaho alaihe wa sallam!*) had made him a *mukatab* and a lot of dirhams had been fixed to be paid in return for mukatibat (which is a mutual agreement between a master and his slave that the later will earn the settled sum, pay it to the aster whereafter he will be free from his bondage). Besides the said sum, Hazrat Salman was also to plant 300 date-palm trees and had to look after them till they bore fruit. The Holy Prophet (*sallallaho alaihe wa sallam!*) took upon himself the task of planting the trees with his own auspicious hands and it was his miracle that within a year the trees began to fructify. One of these trees, however, did not bear fruit; it had been planted by Hazrat Umar (*razi Allaho anho!*).

The Holy Prophet (*sallallaho alaihe wa sallam!*) pulled it out and planted another in its place; though it had been planted out of season, it fructified. This was his second miracle. In the holy Madina the said garden is still known as Salman's Garden.

Note 4:- Hazrat Salman (*razi Allaho anho!*) hailed from Isfahan, a province of Iran. His father was the chief of that place and loved his worthy son very much. Salman studied the Zoroastrian religion so assiduously that he soon became a great scholar and a keeper of the fire-temple. But later on when he embraced Christianity, his father put fetters on his feet and interned him in the house as a prisoner. However, he managed to escape, joined a caravan bound for Syria, suffered many troubles and hardships enroute, became a slave till at last he reached Madina (in search of the last prophet).

Hadith 5:- Hazrat Abd Allah ibn Serjis (*razi Allaho anho!*) reports as follows:- I went to the Holy Prophet's (*sallallaho alaihe wa sallam!*) presence at such a time when the people were present there. I took a round around him like this (he actually demonstrated how he took the round). The Holy Prophet (*sallallaho alaihe wa sallam!*) perceived my intention and removed the sheet of cloth (chadar) from his auspicious body. I saw the Seal of Prophethood which was equal to a fist in size in the middle of the shoulders and had mole-like warts on it.

Then I came in front of him and said; "O Apostle of Allah! May Allah pardon you"! So he said : "May Allah pardon you also"! The people asked me if the Holy Prophet (*sallallaho alaihe wa sallam!*) prayed for my pardon I said that he prayed for me as also for them and said : "Ask pardon for yourself as well as for all other Muslims".

26

Thus the Holy Prophet (*sallallaho alaihe wa sallam!*) used to pray for all the people (Muslims).

* * * * * * * *

27

III

THE DESCRIPTION OF THE HAIR OF THE HOLY PROPHET'S
(sallallaho alaihe wa sallam!)
AUSPICIOUS HAIR

As regards the quantity of Holy Prophet's *(sallallaho alaihe wa sallam!)* hair there are various hadiths, which, even if seen cursorily, appear to be different from one another. But in fact there is no contradiction, because hair are a thing which keep growing. If once the hair reached the lobes of the ears, at another time they looked longer than this, for, provenly, he got his hair cut a few times only. So those who saw his hair after cutting, they described them as short, and those who saw them a long time after hair-cut described them to be long.

Certain ulema have also said that the hair in the front of the head reached upto the ear-lobes, the hair in the middle of the head were longer than them, and the hair in the rear of the head reached upto the shoulders.

Important Clarification:- (1) The Holy Prophet's *(sallallaho alaihe wa sallam!)* auspicious habit was to wear hair. (2) The shaving of the head with a razor after the Migration (Hijrah) in A.H. 6, during the Treaty of Hudaibiyah and in A.H. 7, and while performing the *qaza of umrah* in A.H. 19 in the Hajjat al-wida', is proven. (3) It is an act of sunnah to shave the head after completing the different component items *(arkan)* of the hajj and umrah and it merits greater recompense *(thavab)*. (4) Certain ignorant men consider it meritorious to shave

28

the head at times other than those mentioned above; this is an innovation (bid'ah) and hence improper, because the meriting of recompense on shaving the head is proven from the example of the Holy Prophet (sallallaho alaihe wa sallam!) only after performing the component acts of the hajj and umrah. So the shaving with a razor that certain ignorant men consider to be an act of recompense is a sin. The shaving of the hair is a meritorious act only during the hajj and umrah. To clip the hair or wear them or shave them off after the aforesaid occasions is permissible (ja'iz). To consider a permissible act an act worthy of recompense and to chide one who does not have the hair is prohibited (haram). (5) Certain ignorant men rail at those who wear long hair according to the sunnah practice; this is impermissible. (6) Certain superintendents or seminaries compel students to shave off their heads; this too is impermissible. (7) To consider the shaving of head an act of recompense is the practice of the misguided group of the kharijites and hence it is necessary to shun such thinking. (8) The sunnah-permitted hair can be worn upto the lobes of the ears or, if they have grown, upto the shoulders or above the shoulders. (9) To wear English-type hair is Makruh-e tahrimi (a near-prohibited abomination) for the reason that the Holy Prophet (sallallaho alaihe wa sallam!) has forbidden kaz'a, which means the shaving of a certain part of the head and wearing hair on the other part of it, and the English-cut is exactly this forbidden style (1) It is prohibited (haram) for males to plait pigtails like women. The Holy Prophet (sallallaho alaihe wa sallam!) has cursed those males who try of resemble the females and hence it is not permissible for menfolks to wear pigtails like the womenfolk. (11) To have a half-shorn head is also prohibited.

29

Hadith 1:- Hazrat Anas (*razi Allaho anho!*) reports that the Holy Prophet (*sallallaho alaihe wa sallam!*) hair reached upto the middle of his ears.

Hadith 2:- Hazrat Ayesha (*Razi Allaho Anha!*) reports that she and the Holy Prophet (*sallallaho alaihe wa sallam!*) used to take bath from the same pot and his hair were upto the ears and the middle of his shoulders neither too short nor too long but of a medium length.

Note:- The husband's and wife's bathing together is permissible but the stripping of the clothes by one or both is not proven because Hazrat Ayesha (*Razi Allaho Anha!*) has reported that neither she ever saw the Holy Prophet (*sallallaho alaihe wa sallam!*) *satr* (the hidden parts of the body) nor he ever saw hers. According to Imam Nauwavi, the husband's and wife's bathing together is permissible according to the opinion of all the ulema.

Besides this, other methods too are permissible. The husband may take the bath first and the wife thereafter or vice versa; this is permissible according to the Hanafite, the Shafi'ite and the Malekite ulema but it is not permissible according to the Hanblite creed (*mazhab*).

Hadith 3:- Hazrat Br'a (*razi Allaho anho!*) reports that the Holy Prophet's (*sallallaho alaihe wa sallam!*) was of medium height, his chest was broad and his hair were upto the ear-lobes.

Hadith 4:- Hazrat Qatadah (*razi Allaho anho!*) reports as follows:-

"I asked Hazrat Anas as to how were the Holy Prophet (*sallallaho alaihe wa sallam!*) hair"? He replied; "Neither very curly (like those of the Ethiopians') nor quite straight, but with straightness they were also wavy, reaching upto the lobes of the ears".

Necessary Explanation:- The husband can see the wife's private parts and the wife can see the husband's; to see each other's private parts is permissible but it is not good to do so.

Hadith 5:- Hazrat Ibn Abbas (*razi Allaho anho!*) reports that formerly the Holy Prophet (*sallallaho alaihe wa sallam!*) did not part his hair because the polytheists used to part their hair whereas the scripturaries (*Alh-e-Kitab*) did not do so. The noble habit in the beginning was that in those matters for which no specific commandment had been revealed, he liked to be concordant with the scripturaries. In the later part of this life he used to part his hair.

Necessary Explanation:- Before his death he used to part the hair because permission to do so had been granted by Allah. Hence it is permissible (*ja'iz*) for males to part the hair.

* * * * * * * *

31

IV

THE DESCRIPTION OF THE HOLY PROPHET'S
(sallallaho alaihe wa sallam!)
COMBING

To comb the hair is praiseworthy *(mustahab)*. The Holy Prophet *(sallallaho alaihe wa sallam!)* has encouraged it. He too used to comb his hair.

Hadith 1:- Hazrat Ayesha *(Razi Allaho Anha!)* reports that she used to comb the Holy Prophet *(sallallaho alaihe wa sallam!)* hair, even when she used to be in her period.

Note:- It proves that it is permissible for a wife to serve her husband even during her monthly course.

Hadith 2:- Hazrat Anas *(razi Allaho anho!)* reports that the Holy Prophet *(sallallaho alaihe wa sallam!)* used to apply more oil to his hair and used to comb his beard also. He also used to keep a kerchief over his head so as to save the turban from oil-stains and this piece of cloth used to become like the clothes of an oil-presser.

Note:- This shows his habit of cleanliness that to save his cap and turban from the stains of hair-oil, he used to cover the head with a kerchief.

Hadith 3:- Hazrat Ayesha *(Razi Allaho Anha!)* reports that the Holy Prophet *(sallallaho alaihe wa sallam!*) while making ablution, combing hair, putting on shoes, in fact in all actions, used to keep the right side of his body forward; i.e., he used to begin every work from the right side.

Note:- The essential rule is that every work having honour and nobleness ought to be begun always from the right side and the work that is not noble – for instance, entering a lavatory for passing urine – should be begun from the left side. So, one should, while entering the mosque, put the right foot first and come out of it by putting the left foot first.

Hadith 4:- Hazrat Abd Allah ibn Maghaffal (*razi Allaho anho!*) reports that the Holy Prophet (*sallallaho alaihe wa sallam!*) used to prevent from combing hair but sometimes he did not; if he felt the need for combing hair, he combed, otherwise he did not.

He used to prevent the frequent combing of hair. Qazi Iyaz explains that by 'sometime' is meant 3 days. The Holy Prophet's (*sallallaho alaihe wa sallam!*) forbidding the combing of hair every day, is proven. The ulema have stated that the combing of hair every day, if there is no need of doing so, has been forbidden; however, it matters little if one combs out of necessity, but to be always after combing hair is not good.

Necessary Explanation:- The purpose of the prophetic instruction is to make man realise the value of time and cultivate the dignity of a crusader (*mujahid*), and not to remain busy, like womenfolk, in chevelure, putting up one's hair. Hence, one may comb the hair if it is necessary, but not otherwise.

* * * * * * * *

33

V

THE DESCRIPTION OF THE HOLY PROPHET'S
(sallallaho alaihe wa sallam!)
WHITE HAIR

Hadith 1:- Hazrat Qatadah (*razi Allaho anho!*) reports that he asked Hazrat Anas (*razi Allaho anho!*) whether the Holy Prophet (*sallallaho alaihe wa sallam!*) used to apply hair-dye. He replied that the Holy Prophet's (*sallallaho alaihe wa sallam!*) hair were not greying so much that he would have felt the need of using hair-dye. White hair had appeared only on both the temples. Yes, Hazrat Abu Bakr (*razi Allaho anho!*) used to dye his own hair with henna and katam (a kind of grass).

Note:- To apply black hair-dye is not permissible because its use has been forbidden in hadiths.

Hadith 2:- Hazrat Anas (*razi Allaho anho!*) report that he did not count more than fourteen white hair in the Holy Prophet's (*sallallaho alaihe wa sallam!*) head and the noble beard.

Note:- Here too there is a difference in counting. In certain hadiths the number is 17, in some it is 18 and in others it is 20 also. The implication of all the three statements, however, is that white hair were fewer. It is possible that earlier there were only 14 hair and later on 18 were counted; or there could be difference in counting also. The meaning, however, is to state that white hair were scarce.

Hadith 3:- When someone asked Hazrat Jabir (*razi Allaho anho!*) as to how many of the Holy Prophet's (*sallallaho alaihe wa sallam!*) hair were white, he replied; "When he applied hair-oil, the white hair could not be seen, otherwise some of the hair used to look white".

Note:- When hair-oil is applied, the hair become shiny, and so, due to shining or being set due to applying oil, the few white hair were hidden; and when oil was not applied, the auspicious hair were dishevelled and the white ones amongst them could be sighted and counted.

Hadith 4:- Hazrat Ibn Umar (*razi Allaho anho!*) reports that the Holy Prophet's (*sallallaho alaihe wa sallam!*) white hair were approximately twenty.

Hadith 5:- Hazrat Ibn Abbas (*razi Allaho anho!*) reports that Hazrat Abu Bakr (*razi Allaho anho!*) said" O Apostle of Allah! You have become old". The Holy Prophet (*sallallaho alaihe wa sallam!*) replied; "*Sura-e Hud, Sura-e Waqe'ah, Sura-e Mursalat, Sura-e Amm Yatasa'aloon and Sura-e Izash Shamso Kuwwirat* – these suras have made me old".

Besides these, other suras also which describe the Jehenna and the Day of Judgement are implied. It is stated in other hadith that the Holy Prophet (*sallallaho alaihe wa sallam!*) said; "If you come to know of things that I know, the major part of your time will pass in weeping (and you'll give up laughing), so much so that you'll give up even mating with your wives".

It is stated in *sharh-e Sunnah* that a man saw the Holy Prophet (*sallallaho alaihe wa sallam!*) in dream and asked; "You've stated that Sura-e Hud made you old. So what is that thing in it"? He replied; "There is a verse in it which orders one to be firm and staunch in religion as one ought to be, and to live according to this order". It is obvious that complete steadiness as per this order is very difficult; it is for this reason that the great Sufis have observed that steadiness in religion is superior to a thousand miracles.

Necessary Explanation:- One should tread the straight path strictly in compliance with the order given by Allah to the Holy Prophet (*sallallaho alaihe wa sallam!*) who himself complied fully with the Divine orders. He kept awake at nights in devotions and, having suffered difficulties and hardships had become weak, although he had been endowed with the strength of forty men of Paradise and a man of Paradise will be given the strength of one hundred men of this world. Thus the Holy Prophet (*sallallaho alaihe wa sallam!*) had the strength of four thousand men of the world. Hence the ulema have stated that a man of this world can marry four women. And thus the Holy Prophet (*sallallaho alaihe wa sallam!*) had the strength of living with sixteen thousand women of the world, but notwithstanding all this strength he had become weak.

Hadith 6:- Hazrat Abu Johaifa (*razi Allaho anho!*) reports that the people asked; "O Apostle of Allah! You've become like old men, weak. The signs of old age are visible in you". He replied; "Suras like the Sura-e Hud made me old".

Note:- It is stated in another hadith that once the Holy Prophet (*sallallaho alaihe wa sallam!*) was coming from home. Hazrat Abu Bakr and Hazrat Umar (*razi Allaho anho!*) was sitting in the mosque. The Holy Prophet's (*sallallaho alaihe wa sallam!*) hand was on his beard. Hazrat Abu Bakr said : "May my parents be sacrified over you! O Apostle of Allah! How soon you have become old"! Saying this he began to weep. The Holy Prophet (*sallallaho alaihe wa sallam!*) said : "The suras like the Sura-e Hud have made me old".

Hazrat Abu Bakr's remarks only meant that, looking to his age or strength, his hair should not have become white and yet he looked weak like old men. Allamah Zamakhsari says that he saw a man in the evening with quite black hair but within one night all his hair turned white. Next day when the people asked him about this sudden change, he said : "Last night I saw in dream the grim spectacle of the Day of Judgement when people, handcuffed and fettered, were being thrown into Hell. This scene anguished and upset me so much that all my black hair turned white". *Allaho Akbar!*

Necessary Explanation:- There are several such stories related in books that man becomes old due to extreme anguish and distress. In the case of the Holy Prophet (*sallallaho alaihe wa sallam!*), however, the words "became old" only mean weakness, because white hair he did have were not more than twenty.

Hadith 7:- Hazrat Abu Himsa (*razi Allaho anho!*) reports:- "I, along with my son, went to the Holy Prophet's (*sallallaho alaihe wa sallam!*) presence. The people pointed out to me the place where he was sitting. When I saw him I was convinced that he was a true prophet. At the time there were two pieces of green cloth on his auspicious body and the effect of old age had appeared on some of his hair which were read in colour".

Note:- (1) The two pieces of cloth were a green chadar and a green lungi. (2) Some ulema have stated that those hair were red due to hair-dye and hence the use of hair-dye is permissible, whereas some ulema say that hair turn red before turning white and this redness was an indication that his hair would be white before long. There was awesomeness, lustre and glory of prophetic illumination on the Holy Prophet's (*sallallaho alaihe wa sallam!*) noble, radiant face and hence whosoever happened to glance at him, involuntarily the words escaped from his/her mouth that he was truly a holy prophet.

Hadith 8:- A man asked Hazrat Jabir (*razi Allaho anho!*) whether there was black hair in the Holy Prophet's (*sallallaho alaihe wa sallam!*) head. He replied that some hair in the parting were white but they were hidden when oil was applied.

Necessary Explanation:- On the basis of the aforesaid hadiths the hadith-reporting ulema have stated that the Holy Prophet (*sallallaho alaihe wa sallam!*) in spite of having strength of four thousand men, had become weak, but white hair were not more than 14 to 17 or 20.

They have also stated this reason that white hair generally do not attract women's love. The Holy Prophet's (*sallallaho alaihe wa sallam!*) wives ere comparatively young in age. Since white hair might have caused disinclination, Lord Most High, in view of the holy wives' feminality, though they loved their illustrious husband most sincerely, did not cause more hair to turn grey; and hence the hair were mostly black. (2) It is abominable (*makruh*) to pick up or clip white hair. The prophetic statement is that white hair are a Musalman's light (*Mawahib*, p.44).

* * * * * * *

VI

THE HOLY PROPHET'S
(sallallaho alaihe wa sallam!)
USE OF HAIR-DYE.

Divergent traditions have been reported from the Holy Prophet *(sallallaho alaihe wa sallam!)* on this topic. The using of hair-dye is proved from certain traditions, whereas it is not so proved from others. It is for this reason that the ulema too are divided regarding this matter: whether the use of hair-dye is permissible or not. Imam Tirmizi's opinion is that the Holy Prophet *(sallallaho alaihe wa sallam!)* had never dyed his hair. Many ulema assert that hair-dye should be used; the Hanafite ulema too say the same thing. There are details about this, in the *Durr-e Mukhtar.* That the Holy Prophet *(sallallaho alaihe wa sallam!)* did not used any hair-dye is correct, for it is stated in the *Bukhari Sharif* that there were not more than 17 white hair in his auspicious head and beard.

Imam Shafi'i says that the Holy Prophet *(sallallaho alaihe wa sallam!)* sometime used hair-dye and sometimes did not, and hence the dyeing of hair is an act of sunnah but the use of the black hair-dye is prohibited *(haram)*. According to the Hanafite ulema the use of hair-dye is praise-worthy *(mustahab)* and that of the black hair-dye is abominable *(makruh)*.

Necessary Explanation:- It is permissible to use black hair-dye in certain awkward circumstances but it is prohibited *(haram)* to use black hair-dye in order to deceive a young girl whom one may send a marriage proposal.

Hadith:- Hazrat Abu Himsah (razi Allaho anho!) reports as follows; "I, along with my son, went to the Holy Prophet's (sallallaho alaihe wa sallam!) holy presence. He asked me if it was my son. I said yes. I said; 'Please be a witness that this is my son.' At this the Holy Prophet (sallallaho alaihe wa sallam!) said : 'The retribution of his sin and crime is not upon you and that of yours is not upon him'. I Abu Himsah says that at that time he found some of the Holy Prophet's (sallallaho alaihe wa sallam!) hair to be red.

Note:- (1) It appears from this that some red hair-dye had been used. (2) Prior to Islam, the retribution and punishment for crime was being meted out to one another. It was for this reason that Abu Himsah requested the Holy Prophet (sallallaho alaihe wa sallam!) to be a witness so that, if it so happened, he would pay the retribution. But the Holy Prophet (sallallaho alaihe wa sallam!), in order to abolish this unjust practice of the days of ignorance, told Abu Himsah that his son was not accountable for his (father's) sins, and so the retribution for the father's sins would not be exacted from the son nor of the son from the father.

Necessary Explanation:- Such incidents are often heard that a wayward son borrows two to five hundred rupees in the name of his father and then, leaving home, goes away for sight-seeing. Thereafter the creditor makes a demand from the father and releases the money from him. But the father is not responsible for such borrowing; it is the father's goodness that he pays the amount on behalf of his unworthy children. Boys who go

41

to seminaries for studies often open credit accounts in hotels and shops and the hoteliers and shop-keepers force the guardians to clear the accounts, which is not proper (*ja'iz*), for before giving anything on credit they should have obtained the guardians' permission and agreement; without such agreement the guardians cannot be held responsible. Hence the hoteliers and shop-keepers must obtain first the guardians consent and then open such credit-accounts, as otherwise the guardians cannot be deemed as guarantors.

* * * * * * *

VII

THE HOLY PROPHET'S
(*sallallaho alaihe wa sallam!*)
USE OF COLLYRIUM

To apply collyrium to the eyes is praiseworthy (*mustahab*). Besides the benefit to the eyes, one would also get recompense (*thavab*) for following the prophetic practice.

Hadith 1:- Hazrat Ibn Abbas (*razi Allaho anho!*) relates that the Holy Prophet (*sallallaho alaihe wa sallam!*) has said; "Apply the collyrium of ithmid (a mineral product) to the eyes for it increases the light of the eyes (i.e. strengthens the eye-sight) and also helps the growth of the eye-lashes". Hazrat Ibn Abbas further says that the Holy Prophet (*sallallaho alaihe wa sallam!*) had a kohl-box from which he used to apply collyrium thrice to each eye every night.

Note:- Ithmid is the name of a particular antimony which is reddish-black in colour. The ulema also say that this suggestion for the use of collyrium is meant only for those people to whom it suits, as otherwise the applying of collyrium makes an ailing eye more painful.

The application of collyrium to the eyes at night is beneficial, for it remains in the eyes for a long time and thus reaches slowly in adequate quantity to those parts of the eyes where is necessary for producing more light.

43

There are different traditions regarding the number of times the collyrium-rod should be applied to the eye-rims. It appears from some of them that the Holy Prophet (*sallallaho alaihe wa sallam!*) to apply the collyrium-rod thrice to both the eyes, whereas from some it seems that he used to apply it thrice to the right eye and twice to the left. But here too the traditionists are not divergent, for at time he applied it thrice and at times twice only. However, the number of traditions that show that he used to apply the rod thrice are many, as would appear from the hadiths that follow. Hafiz Ibn Hajar and Mulla Ali Qari have preferred those traditions which indicate that the khol-rod was applied to each eye thrice.

Hadith 2:- It is reported from Hazrat Ibn Abbas (*razi Allaho anho!*) that the Holy Prophet (*sallallaho alaihe wa sallam!*) used to apply the collyrium of ithmid thrice to each eye every night before retiring to bed.

Hadith 3:- Hazrat Jabir (*razi Allaho anho!*) reports that the Holy Prophet (*sallallaho alaihe wa sallam!*) has advised to apply the collyrium of ithmid to the eyes as it increased the light of the eyes and helps grow the eye-lashes.

Hadith 4:- It is reported from Hazrat Ibn Abbas (*razi Allaho anho!*) that the Holy Prophet (*sallallaho alaihe wa sallam!*) said; "Of all your collyrium of ithmid is the best, for it produces light in the yes and grows eye-lashes".

Note:- In all these traditions the persuasion is for the use of ithmid-collyrium but this recommendation is meant only for those eyes to which it may suit; otherwise to certain eye-ailments, this collyrium does not suit may persons. However, the applying of collyrium is an act of sunnah and it is superior to use the ithmid-collyrium, but the act of sunnah is accomplished by using any collyrium.

Necessary Explanation:- The eyes are strengthened by the use of collyrium and the harmful elements that descend into the eyes from the head are removed (*Mawahib-e Ladunniyah*, P.47).

One reason for applying collyrium is beautification, for which purpose, according to the instruction of the Shari'ah, it may be applied during day or at night. The other reason is to strengthen and preserve eye-sight and for this purpose it should be applied at night according to the instruction given in the aforesaid note, for it is an act of Sunnah.

* * * * * *

VIII

REGARDING THE HOLY PROPHET'S
(sallallaho alaihe wa sallam!)
CLOTHES

As regards clothes the ulema have stated that for man some clothes are indispensable (*wajib*), some are praiseworthy (*mustahab*), some prohibited (*haram*), some abominable (*makruh*), and some option (*mubah*). Every man, therefore, should select the praiseworthy type of clothes and abstain from wearing the abominable ones.

The clothes that cover the *satr* are indispensable. On days of Eid good clothes and on Fridays white clothes should be put on, for the Shari'ah has insisted upon this practice and has called it praiseworthy. And the wearing of clothes which the Shari'ah has dissuaded from wearing is abominable. For example, a wealthy man may always wear worn out, torn clothes; this is abominable, for the praiseworthy act for him is to put on such clothes that may indicate the signs of Allah's bounty to him. And to wear such dresses which have been prohibited is unlawful (*haram*); for instance, males may put on silken clothes. This is unlawful, though it is permissible to wear silken clothes as a treatment for some disease. (*Mawahib*, P.50).

Necessary Explanation:- (1) One should wear clothes like the ones worn by the righteous. To wear trousers (pajamas), lungi and shirt that reach upto the middle of the calves is praiseworthy. (2) To wear the typical

46

dresses of other communities that create resemblance with them is *haram* (prohibited). (3) To wear such clothes in which those portions of the body which it is obligatory to hide remain exposed is prohibited; to wear shorts or short drawers is *haram*, for the knees and thigh which it is obligatory to hide remain naked. It becomes unlawful due to omitting an obligatory act. (4) For womenfolk it is *haram* to put on thin clothes through which their bodies remain visible. (5) To wear body-clasping garments whereby certain portions of the female body become prominent is also *haram*. However, the wearing of thin or body-clasping clothes at home is permissible. (6) The wearing of clothes for show-off, self-publicity and flaunting one's status and greatness is also *haram*.

Clarification about Note No. (2):- About eighty, ninety years ago the ulema had issued *fatwas*, declaring the wearing of coat and pant *haram* because it created resemblance with the Britishers; but now that all communities put on this dress, the question of identification with any particular community does not arise, and hence it is now permissible to wear it.

Hadith 1:- It is reported by Hazrat Umm Salmah (*razi Allaho anha!*) that of all clothes the Holy Prophet (*sallallaho alaihe wa sallam!*) liked kurta (long shirt) most.

Note:- The ulema have given different reasons for his liking the kurta most. (1) The whole body is covered fully by the kurta whereas it is not covered adequately by chadar (haick) and lungi. (2) By wrapping oneself in a haick one feels some weight over the body, whereas the kurta is not only light but also cheap. (3) The kurta which covers the *satr* fully also gives a handsome look. It was for such reason that the Holy Prophet (*sallallaho alaihe wa sallam!*) liked the kurta most.

Explanation:- The Holy Prophet (*sallallaho alaihe wa sallam!*) buying a pajamas is proven but his wearing it is not proven. Prophet Hazrat Ibrahim (peace be on him!) was the first man who had put on pajamas, therefore, Prophet Moses (peace be on him!) had put on pajamas while going to Mount Sinai. (*Mawahib*, P.57). The Holy Prophet (*sallallaho alaihe wa sallam!*) throughout his life wore lungi only. The word used (in the tomes of Hadith) for lungi also is 'chadar' which shows that the lungi too was worn unstitched. He used to wear it unstitched only.

Hadith 2:- Similarly some people have reported from Hazrat Umm Slama (*Razi Allaho Anha!*) that the Holy Prophet (*sallallaho alaihe wa sallam!*), for wearing, liked the shirt most.

Note:- Mulla Ali Qari, with reference to Dimyati, has reported that the Holy Prophet's (*sallallaho alaihe wa sallam!*) shirt was of cotton cloth, neither too long nor too short and the sleeves too were not very long. Allamah Baijori has reported that the Holy Prophet (*sallallaho alaihe wa sallam!*) only one shirt. It is related on the authority of Hazrat Ayesha (*Razi Allaho Anha!*) that the Holy Prophet's (*sallallaho alaihe wa sallam!*) noble habit was that he would not save anything from the morning meal for the evening nor from the evening meal for the morning and he would not keep double of anything whether it be clothes, haick or lungi, shirt or a pair of shoes.

It is related from Hazrat Ibn Abbas (*razi Allaho anho!*) that the Holy Prophet's (*sallallaho alaihe wa sallam!*) shirt used to be above his ankles. Hence Allamah Shami writes that the shirt ought to be upto the middle of the calves.

Necessary Explanation:- Any clothes whether it is pajamas or pant, shirt, sherwani (long coat) or gown, that reach below the ankles are *makruh-e tahrimi* (near-prohibited abomination). The prophetic statement, rather warning, is that there are three men who Allah Most High will not pardon on the Day of Judgement nor will look kindly at them. One of these men is the man who might have hung his lungi (or pajamas) down below his ankles out of pride. (*Muslim*) Hence the wearing of pajamas or lungi that may reach below the ankles is prohibited (*haram*) for males. The shirt reaching upto the middles of the calves is praiseworthy (*mustahab*).

Hadith 3:- It is reported from Hazrat Asma (*Razi Allaho Anha!*) that the sleeves of the Holy Prophet's (*sallallaho alaihe wa sallam!*) shirt were upto the wrists.

It is stated in certain traditions that the sleeves reached down below the wrists. Both the kinds of such traditions should be ascribed to different times; or the cloth of the shirt (after two, three days' wear) used to shrink up. When the shirt was worn for the first time, the sleeves must have been long. Or the narrators have described the sleeves by a rough estimate and hence this difference in the length of the sleeves.

Maulana Khalil Ahmad has stated in *Baz'al-majhud* that the hadith that states its being upto the wrists shows that its being upto the wrists is superior (*afzal*) and that it is permissible if it be down below the wrists.

Allamah Jazri has stated that to keep the shirt-sleeves upto the wrists is a prophetic practice (sunnah) and besides this, it is permissible that the sleeves of a gown or a sherwani may be a little down below the carpus but not passing below the fingers.

Necessary Explanation:- (1) Please understand this proposition (mas'ala) that is not permissible for the males to have long sleeves that may go down below the fingers; it will be reckoned as an act of extravagance and hence it is very necessary to avoid it. (2) If the sleeves come upto the wrists, it is very advantageous in saving oneself from heat and cold. (Mawahib, P.51).

Hadith 4:- Hazrat Qurrah ibn Iyas (razi Allaho anho!) states; "I, accompanying a party of the Moazaina tribe, went to the Holy Prophet's (sallallaho alaihe wa sallam!) presence with the intention of paying allegiance to him. At that time the collar of his shirt was open. I, for the sake of acquiring blessing (baraka), inserted may hand in his collar and touched the Seal of Prophethood".

Note:- Every act or aspect of a beloved person becomes admirable. After having seeing the collar open Orwah (razi Allaho anho!), the narrator of this incident, reports that he never saw Qurrah and his son Muawiyah buttoning their shirts and keeping their collars closed, whether the season was hot or severely cold. It is on account of this intense love of the Companions that every aspect and action of the Holy Prophet (sallallaho alaihe wa sallam!) has continued to reach the ummah to date. May Allah Most High bestow good reward upon all of them! Amen!

And may Allah Most High bestow upon us all also the grace to act according to each and every prophetic practice ! Amen!

Hadith 5:- It is reported from Hazrat Anas (*razi Allaho anho!*) that the Holy Prophet (*sallallaho alaihe wa sallam!*), reclining against Hazrat Osamah (*razi Allaho anho!*), came out of his house. He was then wearing a Yemenite embroidered cloth. Having come out of the house, he then led the Companions in prayers.

Note:- This incident took place during the Holy Prophet's (*sallallaho alaihe wa sallam!*) terminal sickness.

Hadith 6:- It is related from Hazrat Abu Sa'eed Khudri (*razi Allaho anho!*) that whenever the Holy Prophet (*sallallaho alaihe wa sallam!*) put on a new dress, he, in order to express his joy, used to pray like this:-

"*Allahumma Iakal-hamdo kama kasautanihey as'aloka khairahu wa khaira ma sune'a lahu wa a'oozobeka min sharrehe wa sharr-e ma sune's lahu*".

"O Allah All praise is for You, and thanks are due to You for this dress You clothed me with. From You alone I seek its goodness and the goodness of the purpose for which it has been made, and I seek protection from its evil and the evil of the purpose for which it has been made".

Note:- The goodness or evil of dress is evident, but the good or evil of the purpose for which it has been made is that it may be used to save oneself from heat and cold and that it may be used for decoration and for

51

devotions to Allah, and may not be used for acts of disobedience, pride, hypocrisy, etc. It is from such acts that he sought divine protection.

Necessary Explanation:- Besides the above, several other invocations too have been related in hadiths and several benefits reciting these invocations have also been reported. It says in one hadith that when one puts on new clothes and recites the invocation, one will remain under Allah's protection and both during life and at the time of death there will be a veil, created by Allah, upon him/her. It is said in one tradition that Allah Most High will pardon all his sins. Similarly, one who sees a person wearing new clothes should bless the wearer. When Hazrat Umar (*razi Allaho anho!*) put on new clothes, the Holy Prophet (*sallallaho alaihe wa sallam!*) blessed him. The holy Companions too (*razi Allaho anho!*) used to invoke longevity of life for the wearer of new clothes. (*mawahib*, P.54).

Hadith 7:- Hazrat Anas (*razi Allaho anho!*) reports that the embroidered chadars of Yemen were liked more by the Holy Prophet (*sallallaho alaihe wa sallam!*).

Note:- This hadith is antithetical to the first hadith. Answer: (1) Chadar and shirt (kurta) both were liked and there is no contradiction if two things are like. (2) For wearing he liked shirt and for covering himself, chadar. (3) Amongst clothes the shirt was liked more for wearing and the chadar was liked more for its green colour, for clothes of green colour are the garments of the occupants of Paradise. This was the main reason he liked the green-coloured chadars of Yemen more.

Necessary Explanation:- (1) The Yemenite chadar was liked more because of its soft texture. (2) The shirt

52

was liked for domestic use, while the haick (chadar) was liked for wrapping himself for the Companions' majlises (assemblies). (3) The haick was also preferred during the winter season.

Hadith 8:- Abu Johaifa (*razi Allaho anho!*) reports that he saw the Holy Prophet (*sallallaho alaihe wa sallam!*) wearing red clothes and "the shine of his calf, as though, is still before my eyes".

Note:- Hazrat Sufyan, the narrator of this hadith, says; "My understanding is that these clothes had red embroidery on them". This opinion of Sufyan is for the reason that the wearing of red clothes by males is prohibited. But Maulana Rashid Ahmad Gungohi says that it is permissible (*ja'iz*) even for menfolks to put on red-coloured clothes, but, for the sake of piety, it is better not to wear such clothes.

Necessary Explanation:- Regarding red clothes Allamah Shami has quoted certain opinions in vol. 5 and has reported that it is *makruh-e tanzihi* (abomination-affecting-purity) for males to wear red clothes.

Hadith 9:- Hazrat Bra' reports that he did not see anyone more handsome in red clothes than the Holy Prophet (*sallallaho alaihe wa sallam!*) and his auspicious hair were reaching his shoulders.

Necessary Explanation:- The ulema also have stated that meaning of this red colour: that these red clothes, shirt and lungi, and red stripes on them.

Hadith 10:- Hazrat Qailah bint Makhzumah (*Razi Allaho Anha!*) has reported that she saw the Holy Prophet (*sallallaho alaihe wa sallam!*) in such condition

53

that there were upon his body two old lungis which had been dyed in saffron but there had remained no trace of saffron on them.

Note:- There is a prohibition too against wearing saffron-dyed clothes and hence the details was given in the hadith that the effect of saffron had disappeared. The Holy Prophet (*sallallaho alaihe wa sallam!*) wrapped himself in old lungis due to his humility and devoutness to Allah. To put on old clothes with such intention merits recompense; similarly, to wear new clothes so as to express thank for Allah's bounties is also meritorious. Seeing fine clothes on the body of an august man, a man in torn and tattered clothes asked him about the dress. The august man replied; "My wearing good clothes is to express thanks for Allah's bounties, while from your wearing ragged clothes people will consider you to be a fakir. Hence your features are like those of a beggar, whereas my fine clothes show me to be a rich man".

Objective:- To put on ordinary clothes for the sake of humility is a meritorious act. Similarly, putting on goods clothes one should express thanks of Allah; or, if a friend has given you a gift of cloth, your friend or relative will be pleased on your wearing its dress, and this, too, therefore, is an act that merits recompense. It is proven from the Holy Prophet (sallallaho alaihe wa sallam!) that once he had bought a suit of clothes in exchange for 27 camels. The Naqshbandiyah, and the Shazliyah ulema consider it good to put on fine clothes so that thanks for Allah's bounties may be expressed and people may not consider them fakirs. There is, however, danger in both the way; putting on goods clothes one should not show pride and in ordinary clothes one should not claim to be a Sufi and an august man.

Imam Abu Hanifa used to put on a haick worth 400 dinars. Similarly, Imam Muhammad too used to wear good clothes and used to say : "I put on such clothes so that the attention of my wives and slaves-maids may not be attracted by others".
(*Fathul-mulhim* vol.i.,p.256).

Hadith 11:- It is reported from Hazrat Fazl ibn Abbas *(razi Allaho anho!)* that the Holy Prophet *(sallallaho alaihe wa sallam!)* said "Adopt white clothes; it is the best attire".

Note:- White clothes should be worn during life time and the dead should be covered with a white shroud. The Holy Prophet's *(sallallaho alaihe wa sallam!)* wearing white clothes is proven from the authentic *(sahih)* tradition of the *Bukhari-Sharif.*

Hadith 12:- The same has been reported from Hazrat Samorah ibn Jundub *(razi Allaho anho!)* also that the Holy Prophet *(sallallaho alaihe wa sallam!)* said : "Put on white clothes and enshroud the dead also in white cloth, for white cloth remains neater and cleaner".

Note:- The meaning of its remaining neat and clean is that if gets stained or soiled, one knows it immediately.

Necessary Explanation:- (1) When the cloth is white, one has to labour more to remove any stain or uncleanliness from it and wherefore there remains no doubt to any trace of uncleanliness. (2) On the basis of the said traditions, it is an act of sunnah to put on white clothes. (3) One should put on white clothes for attending functions, meetings and assemblies, for Friday prayers and for going to any mosque and religious function. Similarly, (4) one should go in white clothes to such assemblies where there may be the presence of angel – for instance, in the assembly for the recitation (*qir'at*) of the Quran, preaching (*wa'z*) and divine remembrance (*zikar*)' (5) One will see angels in the grave and hence the shroud should be white. (6) The best colour for clothes is white, then red, and then yellow (*Mawahib*, p.56). (7) The Holy Prophet's (*sallallaho alaihe wa sallam!*) auspicious habit was that he would always put on ordinary clothes. (8) In those days wool used to be rough and prickly; he used to wear clothes of such rough wool. (9) He did not insist upon wearing any particular kind of clothes, he would put on any clothes available at the time. (1) Similarly, he did not insist on any particular colour (11) nor he had any fondness for any particular style. (12) Once he had put on a narrow-sleeved grown in a journey. (13) His buying a costly cloth in return for 27 or 30 camels is proven; hence the buying of costly cloth is permissible (for the *ummah*). (14) It is also permissible to put on clothes that may have been woven and stitched by infidels. (15) The meaning of "Byzantine gown" has been explained to be any style that may not be the national custom of any community; it is permissible to wear this kind of clothes. If one is certain about the presence of any unclean substance in cloth manufactured by Jews and Christians, it is not permissible to wear it.

IX

THE HOLY PROPHET'S
(sallallaho alaihe wa sallam!)
LIVELIHOOD

Under this heading have been described hadiths to show how simple was the Holy Prophet's (sallallaho alaihe wa sallam!) life and with what privations he lived it. Hadiths quoted under another heading that will come shortly will show what things he used in his straitened circumstances.

Hadith 1:- Ibn Srin (Allah's mercy be on him!) reports as follows :-

Once we were sitting with Hazrat Abu Huraira (razi Allaho anho!) who was attired in an ocher-coloured lungi and chadar. Abu Huraira wiped his nose with another lungi of that cloth and began to say with astonishment to himself; "Allah! Allah! O Abu Huraira ! You wipe your nose with a fine linen (katan)! There was a time when you used to lie unconscious between the Holy Prophet's (sallallaho alaihe wa sallam!) room and the people, considering you to be mad, used to step on your neck while crossing. Though you were not mad, such used to be your condition due to hunger".

Note:- Katan was considered a good cloth in those days for its thinness. The Companions, while going out of the mosque, used to step on Abu Huraira's neck for the reason that in those days the treatment for lunatic was believed to be this only that some pressure should be put on their necks. The purpose of narrating this story in the Holy Prophet's (sallallaho alaihe wa

57

sallam!) life is that Abu Huraira was one of the Companions of the Table (Suffa) and whatever the Holy Prophet (*sallallaho alaihe wa sallam!*) received, he used to send it first of all to these destitute Companions. The starvation of the Companions of the Suffa and their unconsciousness or stupor due to intense hunger which made them look like mad persons, shows that the Holy Prophet (*sallallaho alaihe wa sallam!*) often did not have anything to feed these Companions.

It is reported from Hazrat Abu Huraira (*razi Allaho anho!*) that he asked Hazrat Umar (*razi Allaho anho!*) the meaning of a Quranic verse. Hazrat Umar was explaining it while walking but Abu Huraira could not continue to walk along with him; he fainted and fell down due to acute hunger.

Today there is much hue and cry amongst the Muslims about financial stringency. The problem of bread for them is so important that every kind of irreligiousness is accepted for its sake. But when we cast a look at the Companions' lives, even one-tenth of their privations is not seen in ours. Notwith-standing their hardships and pangs of hunger the Companions did not lag behind in making inquiries about religious matters. The thought and question of bread was conspicuously absent in their lives; they did not mar their religion for the sake of worldly gains.

Necessary Explanation:- The Companions of the Suffa were those people who had dedicated themselves to the acquisition of religious knowledge at the Holy Prophet's (*sallallaho alaihe wa sallam!*) feet. He used to look after all their needs. Today we call such an institution a madrasah, a (dar al-ulum suminary) or a khanqah (hospice).

Abu Huraira was a student of those early days; he, in spite of suffering the said hardships, used to acquire knowledge and had thus become an outstanding remembrancer (*hafiz*) of hadiths. More than five thousand hadiths have been recorded in books from him. From the description of the straitened circumstances of the students of those days one can ascertain the financial stringency and distress of their great, affectionate and sympathetic teacher, the Holy Prophet (*sallallaho alaihe wa sallam!*), who would not eat before feeding them. It is for this reason that Imam Tirmizi has included this seemingly inappropriate hadith about the Ahl-e Suffa in describing the Holy Prophet's (*sallallaho alaihe wa sallam!*) personal circumstances.

Hadith 2:- Malik ibn Dinar (Allah's mercy be on him!) says that the Holy Prophet (*sallallaho alaihe wa sallam!*) never ate bread or mutton to his fill, except at a *zifaf*. Malik bin Dinar says that when he asked the meaning of zifaf from a bedouin, the latter replied; "To dine with others".

Note:- Certain ulema have stated that the Holy Prophet (*sallallaho alaihe wa sallam!*) ate to his fill only in feasts but it happened rarely. But other ulema reject this statement and assert that he used to eat to his fill only as a host; i.e., whenever he threw a party or guests came to his place, he used to give them company till the end so that none of them might rise up hungry, but it is obvious that the guests cannot go on eating if the host withdraws his hand. But even this eating to his fill, wherever it is mentioned, only means that he ate to fill his only 2/3 of his belly.

* * * * * *

59

X

THE DESCRIPTION OF THE HOLY PROPHET'S
(sallallaho alaihe wa sallam!)
S O C K S

It is proven that he wore several kinds of socks. The good manner of putting on socks is that the right sock should be put on first, but before putting it on, it should first be shaken off, because Tabrani, under the heading 'Miracles', has recorded a hadith from Ibn Abbas regarding this. Once the Holy Prophet (*sallallaho alaihe wa sallam!*) was in a jungle. He put on one sock and while he was still thinking of putting on the other a crow snatched it away in a fell swoop. Having flown high, it threw it down. When the sock touched the ground, a snake emerged from it. The Holy Prophet (*sallallaho alaihe wa sallam!*) thanked Allah and made a rule that socks must be shaken off before wearing.

Necessary Explanation:- In this story the socks are leather-socks. In countries where the winters are very severe people put on leather socks to cover cotton, woollen or nylon stocks. (2) The proposition (*mas'ala*) regarding the drawing of hand (*masah*) over socks is that it is permissible over the said leather-socks with certain conditions, but to do so over nylon or woollen socks is not permissible.

Hadith 1:- Hazrat Buraidah (*razi Allaho anho!*) reports that King Negus had sent a present of a pair of simple, black socks to the Holy Prophet (*sallallaho alaihe wa sallam!*). He put them on and, while making ablution (*wuzu*), also drew his hand over them.

Negus (Najashi) was the title of the king of Ethiopia. His name was As'hamah and he had embraced Islam at the Holy Prophet's (*sallallaho alaihe wa sallam!*) invitation.

The ulema have inferred from this hadith that it is permissible to accept the present of an infidel.

Hadith 2:- It is reported from Hazrat Moghirah ibn Sho'abah (*razi Allaho anho!*) that Dehye Kalabi had made a present of a pair of socks to the Holy Prophet (*sallallaho alaihe wa sallam!*) (in another tradition there is mention of socks as well as a gown). The Holy Prophet (*sallallaho alaihe wa sallam!*) put them on and used to wear them so much that at last they were worn out.

* * * * * *

XI

THE DESCRIPTION OF
THE HOLY PROPHET'S
(sallallaho alaihe wa sallam!)
AUSPICIOUS SANDALS

Shaikh al-Hadith Maulana Zakariya Sahib has translated the word 'na'l' in very hadith as 'shoes', but I have translated it as 'chappals' (sandals), because the two-strap style described in the *Mawahib* clearly indicates that they were chappals and not shoes. Perhaps because in Uttar Pradesh and other states of India also even chappals are called shoes, the Shaikh al-Hadith has translated *na'l* as shoes.

Note:- A sketch of the auspicious chappals and their merits and blessings have been given in details in Zad al-Sa'eed by Maulana Ashraf Ali Thanvi. Their properties are endless; the ulema have experienced them many a time. He says that by keeping a copy of this sketch with oneself, one is blessed with the Holy Prophet's (*sallallaho alaihe wa sallam!*) *ziyarat* (vision), is released from the clutches of oppressors, achieves universal popularity and success in every goal through the mediation (*tawwasul*) of these auspicious chappals. The method of seeking *tawwasul* is also given in that small booklet.

Hadith 1:- Hazrat Qatadah (*razi Allaho anho!*) reports that he asked Hazrat Anas (*razi Allaho anho!*) as to how the Holy Prophet's (*sallallaho alaihe wa sallam!*) chappals were and he replied; "In-each chappal there were two straps". A similar hadith has been reported from Hazrat Abu Huraira also.

In Arabia the chappals used to be different from the ones we find today. There used to be two straps fastened over a leather-sole and these were called *na'l*, like the slippers of today, for in those days there were no shoes of the type we use in modern times.

Hadith 2:- Hazrat Ibn Abbas (*razi Allaho anho!*) reports that there were double straps in the Holy Prophet's (*sallallaho alaihe wa sallam!*) chappals.

Note:- the name of one of the narrators of this hadith is Hazza (meaning 'a cobbler'). He was in fact not a cobbler but because of his keeping company with a cobbler, he too was nicknamed cobbler, for one cannot escape the effect of the company one keeps.

Necessary Explanation:- In the present age parents do not look after their children properly; they do not care at all where and with whom their children associate. The great Persian sage, Shaikh Sa'di, said axiomatically that the company of the virtuous makes one virtuous and that of evil-doers makes one an evil-doer. Prophet Noah's (peace be on him!) son kept company with the infidels and smirched the reputation of the prophetic family, whereas a dog associated with the Companions of the Cave (*Ashab-e Kahf*) and became a man (i.e. as virtuous as a man). This dog (Qitmir by name) has been described in the Holy Quran. The moral is that one should always keep the company of the good and insist upon the children also to keep company with the virtuous.

Hadith 3:- Isa ibn Tohman reports that "Hazrat Ans (*razi Allaho anho!*) took out a pair of chappals and showed it to us; there were no hair upon them". Then Isa adds that Thabit told him that these were the Holy Prophet's (*sallallaho alaihe wa sallam!*) chappals.

Note:- The Arabs, by and large, while manufacturing chappals, did not remove hair from the hide, and hence the narrator has stated that the Holy Prophet's (*sallallaho alaihe wa sallam!*) were without hair, as has been stated in the following hadith as well.

Hadith 4:- Hazrat Obayd ibn Joriyah (*razi Allaho anho!*) asked Hazrat Ibn Umar (*razi Allaho anho!*); "Why do you wear hairless chappals?" "I have seen", replied he, "the Holy Prophet (*sallallaho alaihe wa sallam!*) wearing similar chappals and also performing ablution wearing the same, and hence I prefer hairless chappals".

Note:- The meaning of performing ablution wearing chappals is that the shoes of those days were like chappals and hence the feet could be washed without inconvenience while wearing them or it means that the chappals could be put on easily immediately after ablution. Both these things are permissible and it was to demonstrate this permission that the Holy Prophet (*sallallaho alaihe wa sallam!*) used to perform ablution like this.

Necessary Explanation:- Hazrat Abd Allah ibn Umar's (*razi Allaho anho!*) deep love for the Holy Prophet (*sallallaho alaihe wa sallam!*) and his conformance with his manners is indicated that he used to wear the same kind of chappals he had seen his beloved Prophet (*sallallaho alaihe wa sallam!*).

Hadith 5:- Hazrat Amr bin Horais (*razi Allaho anho!*) reports that he saw the Holy Prophet (*sallallaho alaihe wa sallam!*), saying prayer (salat) wearing such chappals in which another piece of leather was protrudent.

Note:- That is, either the sole had double leather or a broken strap had been reinforced with another piece of leather.

Hadith 6:- Hazrat Abu Huraira (*razi Allaho anho!*) reports that the Holy Prophet (*sallallaho alaihe wa sallam!*) said; "Let no one walk wearing only one chappal; either put off both the chappals".

Note:- From this hadith is known the Holy Prophet's (*sallallaho alaihe wa sallam!*) habit that he never walked wearing only one chappal.

Necessary Explanation:- There are several expediencies in the Holy Prophet's (*sallallaho alaihe wa sallam!*) forbidding this odd practice. (1) The said practice does not look good. (2) It causes inconvenience in walking. (3) There remains no balance in steps and hence there is apprehension of tripping and sprain. (4) The Holy Prophet (*sallallaho alaihe wa sallam!*) sometimes used to walk bare-footed also, particularly when he went for devotions. (5) The style of two straps consisted in having one strap between the toe and its adjacent finger and the other in between the middle and the adjoining fingers (Mawahib p.60).

The order contained in this hadith ought to be made a regular habit, of course, it matters little if one puts on a single chappal or shoe due to some excuse or a particular reason. The most important thing is that there should be no immorality or incivility in any matter; and every thing is done according to its mode and method. This is the reason that the ulema have forbidden the wearing of only one sleeve or one sock;

either one puts on both the sleeves or both the stocks or puts of both.

Hadith 7:- It is reported from Hazrat Jabir (*razi Allaho anho!*) that the Holy Prophet (*sallallaho alaihe wa sallam!*) has forbidden to eat with the left hand and put the chappal or shoe on the left foot first.

Necessary Explanation:- Because of this command, it is abominable to eat with the left hand and to start wearing anything from the left side.

Hadith 8:- It is reported from Hazrat Abu Huraira (*razi Allaho anho!*) that the Holy Prophet (*sallallaho alaihe wa sallam!*) said; "When one wants to put on shoes, let one begin doing so with the right foot and when one puts them off, let one do so with the left foot. So, while wearing, the right foot should be the first, and while putting off, the left foot should precede.

Note:- The rule is that whichever thing is worn for decoration, it is praiseworthy (*mustahab*) to put it on from the right side; one should put on pajamas, lungi, shirt, coat, sweater, etc., from the right side first.

Necessary Explanation:- While coming out of the mosque, it is praiseworthy to take out the left foot first. So, put the left foot first on the chappal, than take out the right foot, put on the chappal and then put on the left chappal.

Hadith 9:- Hazrat Ayesha (*razi Allaho anha!*) reports that the Holy Prophet (*sallallaho alaihe wa sallam!*) used to begin, as far, as possible, from the right side in combing hair, wearing shoes, making ablution, in almost every thing. From the phrase "as far as possible" it appears that if one begins it with the left side or foot due to some disability or excuse, it is of no consequence.

Necessary Explanation:- The praiseworthy act is that while putting off shoes or chappals, one should begin from the left side, and while putting on, one begins with the right side.

Hadith 10:- Hazrat Abu Huraira (*razi Allaho anho!*) reports that there were two straps in the Holy Prophet's (*sallallaho alaihe wa sallam!*) chappals. Similarly, the chappals worn by Hazrat Abu Bakr (*razi Allaho anho!*) and Hazrat Umar (*razi Allaho anho!*) also had two straps. The style of having one strap was begun by Hazrat Usman (*razi Allaho anho!*).

Necessary Explanation:- (1) Hazrat Usman's (*razi Allaho anho!*) doing so was for the reason that the people might not consider it necessary to have two straps. (2) For *na'l* it is stated in the *Lam'e al-durari* (vol.i, p.86) also that there is difference between the Arabian and the Indian types, in Arabia *na'l* means chappal and in India it means shoes.

One strap is not abominable. In those days the custom was to have two straps and so the Holy Prophet (*sallallaho alaihe wa sallam!*) also had made a pair having two straps.

* * * * * *

67

XII

THE DESCRIPTION OF THE HOLY PROPHET'S
(sallallaho alaihe wa sallam!)
RING

Hadith 1:- Hazrat Anas (razi Allaho anho!) has reported that the Holy Prophet's (sallallaho alaihe wa sallam!) ring was made of silver and its stone was Ethiopian.

Note:- It is permissible, according to all the ulema, to wear a silver ring, but it is impermissible to wear a ring made of iron, steel, copper or brass.

The Holy Prophet (sallallaho alaihe wa sallam!) had no ring in the beginning of his career, but when he came to know that kings did not give any importance to letters on which the sender's seal was not set, he got a signet-ring prepared when, in A.H.6, he began sending letters to rulers and kings, inviting them to embrace Islam.

Note:- There is divergence of opinion among the ulema regarding the wearing of ring. Some ulema assert that it is an act of sunnah, whereas others say that except a king and a judge it is abominable for others to wear a ring. According to the Hanafite ulema, it is an act of sunnah for a judge, a ruler and a mutawalli (superintendent) to use a ring because they need it by reason of their offices; besides them, though it is permissible for others also who do not require it for the purpose of correspondence, etc., to wear it, it is not very good for them, because the Holy Prophet (sallallaho

68

alaihe wa sallam!) also had got a signet-ring prepared due to necessity. Moreover, there is a tradition in the *Abu Da'ud Sharif* to the effect that the Holy Prophet (*sallallaho alaihe wa sallam!*) has forbidden the wearing of ring. On the other hand, the evidence of many Companions' wearing rings as well as of permission for wearing it is also found in several hadiths. However, one will have to consider the restriction superior that it is not good to wear a ring without necessity.

Necessary Explanation:- (1) To wear rings with the motive of flaunting and putting on airs and gaining notability is forbidden. (2) Ibn Arabi (Allah's mercy be on him!) writes that the custom of making signet-rings already existed in the former nations and in Islam too it is an act of sunnah. (3) The act of sunnah will be discharged if one borrows a ring from other or takes on rent for wearing, but it is superior to put on one of one's own ownership. (4) Allamah Zain al-Din Iraqi (Allah's mercy be on him!) writes that it has not been established whether the Holy Prophet's (*sallallaho alaihe wa sallam!*) signet-ring was square, triangular or round; so the sunnah will be discharged if one puts on a ring of any shape.

Hadith 2:- It is reported from Hazrat Abd Allah ibn Umar (*razi Allaho anho!*) that the Holy Prophet (*sallallaho alaihe wa sallam!*) had got prepared a silver ring with which he used to set his seal on letters, but he did not wear it.

Note:- The Holy Prophet's (*sallallaho alaihe wa sallam!*) wearing a ring is proven from a good many hadiths and hence the ulema have explained away the above-mentioned hadith much. (1) The Holy Prophet (*sallallaho alaihe wa sallam!*) did not wear it always. (2) Some ulema assert that he had two rings, one for sealing and the other for wearing. (3) It says in one hadith that he used to wear the ring in the right hand. Once his eyes fell on the ring during prayer and he gave up wearing it. Since the ring was a thing of necessity, it was difficult to give it up altogether; even so he had given up wearing it for most of the time.

Explanation:- Ponder over the instruction implied in it: a thing of necessity ought to be used only in order to fulfil a need.

Hadith 3:- Hazrat Anas (*razi Allaho anho!*) reports that the Holy Prophet's (*sallallaho alaihe wa sallam!*) ring was of silver and its bezel too was of silver.

Note:- This hadith is contradictory to the first one in which the bezel is said to have been Ethiopian. If it be so, then. according to the opinion of those people who believe that there were two rings, no question arises. But those who believe the there was only one ring they state that the bezel was Ethiopian for it was black in colour or it was negroid or its maker was an Ethiopian. It is better to assume that there were two rings, one of which the Holy Prophet (*sallallaho alaihe wa sallam!*) himself had got prepared and the other had been given him as a present by his Companions. Thus both the hadiths about the signet-ring will be reconciled and there will remain no divergence of opinion.

Allamah Baihaqi's opinion too is the same, as also that of Maulana Shaikh al-Hadith Sahib, that there were two rings.

Hadith 4:- It is reported from Hazrat Anas (*razi Allaho anho!*) that when the Holy Prophet (*sallallaho alaihe wa sallam!*) thought of writing letters to the kings the people told him that the kings did not accept letters without official seal, and so he got a signet-ring prepared "the whiteness of which is still present in my eyes".

Note:- The meaning of this clause in the inverted comas is that 'I remember this matter accurately and the whiteness of the signet-ring is still before my eyes'. There is also a hint in it that the signet-ring was made of silver.

Hadith 5:- It is reported from Hazrat Anas (razi Allaho anho!) that the engraving on his holiness's ring was "MUHAMMAD RASUL ALLAH", Muhammad in one line, Rasul in another and Allah in still another: Allah's Holy Name in the first line, Rasul in the second and Muhammad in the third. The engraving was as under :-

ALLAH RASUL MUHAMMAD

Necessary Explanation:- Muhammadur Rasul Allah: Muhammad is Allah's messenger. But due to respect, Allah was engraved above, messenger in the middle and the auspicious name Muhammad below.

Hadith 6:- It is reported from Hazrat Anas (razi Allaho anho!) that when the Holy Prophet (sallallaho alaihe wa sallam!) though of writing letters to Caesar, Kisra and Negus, the people informed him that those persons did not accept unsealed letters and so he got a ring prepared. Its bezel was of silver in which Muhammad Rasul Allah had been engraved. Kisra was the title of the king of Fars (Persia), Caeser of the king of Rum (Byzantium) and Negus of the king of Ethiopia.

Note:- The Holy Prophet (sallallaho alaihe wa sallam!) had sent his holy letter to Kisra with Hazrat Abd Allah ibn Hazaifa (Razi Allaho anho!). Kisra (Khusrau Parveez) tore off this letter and thus insulted it. When Holy Prophet (sallallaho alaihe wa sallam!)

was informed of this scornful incident, he invoked curses upon Kisra, saying; "May Allah shatter his country to pieces even as he tore off my letter to pieces"! As a result of this curse, Iran was balkanised and lost its sovereignty within short time.

The king of Byzantium received the prophetic letter through Hazrat Dehye ibn Kalabi (*razi Allaho anho!*). Though he was aware of the office of prophethood, he did not believe; however he preserved the auspicious letter with respect.

To Negus had gone Hazrat Umar ibn Umayyah (*Razi Allaho anho!*) with the holy letter. The Negus for whom the Holy Prophet (*sallallaho alaihe wa sallam!*) had performed funeral service was a different person, and this was another Negus to whom the letter was address. According to Mulla Ali Qari, it is not known whether this Negus accepted Islam or not.

The contents of the prophetic letter to Kisra were as under :

"In the Name of Allah, the Compassionate, the Merciful. From Allah's messenger Muhammad to Kisra, who is the great chief of Iran.

"Peace be upon one who adopts guidance and believes in Allah and His messenger, and confesses that none besides Allah is the deity and that Muhammad is Allah's slave and messenger. I invite you towards Allah's call, i.e., the Kalimah, for the reason that I am that messenger of Allah who has been sent to the world to warn those people whose hearts are alive and in order that Allah's argument may be completed for the unbelievers. If you accept Islam, there will be peace; otherwise the crime of the Magians who follow you will also be on you :

72

Kisra tore off this letter and scattered it to the winds and hence his great empire, which was the most powerful in those days, went to wreck and ruin.

Necessary Explanation:- It was, as hinted above, Khusrau Parveez, who had disdainfully torn and insulted the auspicious prophetic letter. His son, Shiruyah, fell in love with his own step-mother and killed his father. The father who had already perceived it, had put a bottle of poison with a label that indicated that it was an aphrosidiac, in the safe. Shiruyah, taking it to be a good medicine, drank it and died. (Thereafter the throne of Iran changed hands rapidly – as many as 14 persons including one or two ladies came on the throne – until, in Hazrat Umar's time, this oldest and the mightiest empire came to an end.

During this fast deteriorating condition of Iran, when a woman was installed on the ancient Iranian throne, the Holy Prophet (*sallallaho alaihe wa sallam!*) remarked; "The nation that charges its affairs to a woman can never become successful".

The letter addressed to the potentate of Byzantium was as under :

"In the Name of Allah, the Compassionate, the Merciful. From Muhammad, who is Allah's slave and messenger, to Heraclius, who is the great one (and Chief) of Byzantium. Peace is for one who adopts guidance. After divine eulogy and greeting, I invite you towards Allah's word (the Kalimah, i.e.,. La ilaha illallaho Muhammadur Rasul Allah). If you accept Islam, you will live peacefully and Allah will bestow double recompense upon you; and if you turn your face from the invitation, the crime of those

73

cultivators who are subordinate to you will be on you. O Scripturaries! Come towards the word that is common between us and you, and that is Divine Unity (Kalima-e Tauhid) so that we do not worship anyone but Allah nor make Allah's partners nor make each other our deity. If, even after this the scripturaries do not believe, then, O Muslims! tell them to be witnesses that we are Muslims" (i.e., we declare our cult openly; now you may do whatever you like).

The Byzantine preserved the letter respectfully and so his kingdom remained intact, but for the fear of losing his kingship, he did not embrace the faith.

The third auspicious letter, described in this hadith, had been addressed to the king of Ethiopia (Abyssinia). Some ulema say that he has already become a Muslim and others say that he embraced Islam after receiving this letter and he died during the Holy Prophet's (*sallallaho alaihe wa sallam!*) time, and a similar letter was also sent to his successor but it could not be known whether the latter became a Muslim or not.

The description of this letter is proven both from books of hadith and books of history and there are many details about it.

Necessary Explanation:- (1) The non-Muslims should first be invited to accept faith and Islam before waging jihad. (2) If correspondence is made with the leaders of non-Muslims, it is proper (ja'iz) to write their titles, official designation, etc. (3) The sin of keeping the subjects on the wrong path will be attributed to the ruler also. (4) The Holy Prophet (*sallallaho alaihe wa sallam!*) had been sent as a prophet for the whole world. (5) The punishment for causing humiliation and disrespect to

74

and scoffing at prophets and saints is meted out very promptly.

Hadith 7:- It is reported from Hazrat Anas (*razi Allaho anho!*) that the Holy Prophet (*sallallaho alaihe wa sallam!*) used to remove his ring while going to the privy.

Necessary Explanation:- The reason for this was that his holy name was engraved on the ring and hence the ulema too have ruled that it is abominable (*Makruh*) to go to a water-closet or latrine wearing a ring on which Allah's holy name may have been inscribed; it is also abominable to go to w.c. with an amulet bearing Allah's name.

Hadith 8:- It is reported from Hazrat Anas (*razi Allaho anho!*) that the Holy Prophet's (*sallallaho alaihe wa sallam!*) ring remained in his hand, then in the hand of Hazrat Umar (*Razi Allaho anho!*), and then in that of Hazrat Usman (*razi Allaho anho!*). The inscription of this ring was: Muhammad Rasul Allah. But in the latter's time it fell into a well.

Note:- The name of the well situated near the Masjid-e Qoba is Arees. During Hazrat Usman's time this holy ring remained in his hand for six years. Then accidentally it fell into the said well. By Hazrat Usman's order water was drawn out from the well continuously for three days, but even after much search and toil it could not be retrieved. Political and religious mischiefs began soon after the disappearance of this holy and auspicious ring.

Necessary Explanation:- (1) The wearing of a ring of any metal except that of silver is impermissible for males. (2) For females too rings of any metal except

75

those of gold and silver are impermissible. (3) Besides rings of gold and silver, other ornaments like bangles, wristlets, anklets, earrings, necklace, etc. are permissible for womenfolk. (4) Chains of brass, copper and steel are permissible for both men and women.

* * * * * *

XIII

THE DESCRIPTION OF THE HOLY PROPHET'S
(sallallaho alaihe wa sallam!)
WEARING THE RING IN THE RIGHT HAND

In the preceding chapter has been described what kind of ring it was and in this we describe the method of wearing it.

Hadith 1:- Hazrat Ali (*razi Allaho anho!*), reports that the Holy Prophet (*sallallaho alaihe wa sallam!*) used to wear the ring in the right hand.

Note:- The wearing of the ring both in the right and the left hands is indicated by the traditions, but most ulema have given preference to those traditions that indicate the wearing of the ring in the right hand. There is difference of opinion even amongst the Hanafite ulema: some of them show the wearing of the ring in the right hand to be superior and some in the left hand. It is Allamah Shami who has reported the above two statements, while Imam Nauwavi has reported the consensus of all the ulema on wearing the ring in both the hands without any abomination (*Karahat*).

It has been reported in the *Durr-e Mukhtar* from Quhistani that the wearing of the ring in the right hand is the method of the Rawafiz (the Seceders), and hence one should avoid it; but the author of the *Durr-e Mukhtar* himself has stated that this was an earlier practice which is now extinct.

Maulana Rasheed Ahmed Gungohi has stated that the wearing of the ring in the left hand is the Rawafiz's practice and hence it is abominable. Maulana Khalil Ahmed Saharanpuri says in his *Bazl-al Majhud* that though there is divergence of opinion regarding the Rawafiz's being infidels, there is no divergence regarding their being sinful (*fasiq*), and hence one should save oneself from resemblance with the sinful.

Necessary Explanation:- (1) So, it will be superior to wear the ring in the right hand. (2) Some ulema adduce it as an argument in favour of wearing the watch also in the right hand which is not correct. In my humble opinion, it is harmful for the watch itself, for man usually does more work with the right hand and the frequent movements of the hand can disturb the delicate mechanism of the watch. Hence it is not correct to adduce an argument for the wearing of the watch from the said hadiths.

Hadith 2:- Hazrat Hammad ibn Salmah reports that he saw Abd ar-Rahman bin Abi Raf'e wearing a ring in the right hand. "When I asked him (Ibn Abi Raf'e), he said that he had seen Abd Allah bin Ja'far wearing the ring in the right hand, and Ibn Ja'far used to say that he had seen the Holy Prophet (*sallallaho alaihe wa sallam!*) wearing the ring in the right hand".

Hadith 3:- It is reported from Hazrat Abd Allah bin Ja'far (*razi Allaho anho!*) also that the Holy Prophet (*sallallaho alaihe wa sallam!*) used to wear the ring in the right hand.

Note:- In one hadith it is also reported along with this that decoration is more suitable for the right hand.

Maulana Rasheed Ahmed Gungohi has stated that the wearing of the ring in the left hand is the Rawafiz's practice and hence it is abominable. Maulana Khalil Ahmed Saharanpuri says in his *Bazl-al Majhud* that though there is divergence of opinion regarding the Rawafiz's being infidels, there is no divergence regarding their being sinful (*fasiq*), and hence one should save oneself from resemblance with the sinful.

Necessary Explanation:- (1) So, it will be superior to wear the ring in the right hand. (2) Some ulema adduce it as an argument in favour of wearing the watch also in the right hand which is not correct. In my humble opinion, it is harmful for the watch itself, for man usually does more work with the right hand and the frequent movements of the hand can disturb the delicate mechanism of the watch. Hence it is not correct to adduce an argument for the wearing of the watch from the said hadiths.

Hadith 2:- Hazrat Hammad ibn Salmah reports that he saw Abd ar-Rahman bin Abi Raf'e wearing a ring in the right hand. "When I asked him (Ibn Abi Raf'e), he said that he had seen Abd Allah bin Ja'far wearing the ring in the right hand, and Ibn Ja'far used to say that he had seen the Holy Prophet (*sallallaho alaihe wa sallam!*) wearing the ring in the right hand".

Hadith 3:- It is reported from Hazrat Abd Allah bin Ja'far (*razi Allaho anho!*) also that the Holy Prophet (*sallallaho alaihe wa sallam!*) used to wear the ring in the right hand.

Note:- In one hadith it is also reported along with this that decoration is more suitable for the right hand.

Hafiz Ibn Hajar, who is an Imam in the discipline of Hadith, writes that if one wears it for the sake of embellishment, one should wear it in the right hand, and if it is worn as a signet-ring, it is better to wear it in the left hand.

Hadith 4:- Hazrat Selt ibn Abd Allah (*razi Allaho anho!*) reports that Hazrat Ibn Abbas (*Razi Allaho anho!*) used to wear the ring in the right hand, "and, as far as I remember, he used to say that the Holy Prophet (*sallallaho alaihe wa sallam!*) too used to wear the ring in the right hand".

Note:- There is an additional report in the Abu Da'ud that he used to wear in the first finger, keeping the bezel up. But it is stated in *Bazl-al Majhud,* with reference to *Mirqat al-sa'ood*, that it is more correct to keep the bezel towards the palm, as there is more safety in this method for the bezel too, as reported in many traditions. Allamah Nauwavi too has stated it to be more correct, adding that there is more safety in this method from pride; moreover, he has also reported consensus on its being a sunnah to wear the ring in the last finger. Allamah Shami says that the ring should be worn in the last finger only and while the males should keep the bezel towards the palm, the females may keep it up for the sake of embellishment.

Necessary Explanation:- (1) A wrist-watch is a necessity and so menfolks should keep the dial towards the palm. (2) Since womenfolk wear it for beauty and embellishment, they may keep it outward.

Hadith 5:- Hazrat Imam Muhammad Baqir says that Hazrat Imam Hasan and Hazrat Imam Husain (*razi Allaho anhuma!*) used to wear the ring in their left hands.

80

Note:- This hadith contradicts Imam Tirmizi's heading of this chapter which says that the Holy Prophet (*sallallaho alaihe wa sallam!*) used to wear the ring in the right hand. The explanation, according to Maulana Shaikh al-Hadith Zakariya Sahib, is that the purpose of quoting such hadiths, when numerous hadiths are against them, is to throw a hint regarding their 'weakness'; the specific mention of the right hand in the heading is for the sake of stating superiority and the inclusion of this kind of traditions is to imply permission (*jawaz*). Or, as some great scholars have explained, the words "OR THE LEFT HAND" have been omitted in the heading as per the traditionists' habit. If this explanation is taken to be correct, then the inclusion of the traditions regarding the left hand will not be inappropriate.

Necessary Explanation:- Thereafter both kinds of traditions were reproduced to prove that the Holy Prophet (*sallallaho alaihe wa sallam!*) used to wear the ring in both the hands, sometimes in the right and sometimes in the left.

Hadith 6:- It is reported from Hazrat Ibn Umar (*razi Allaho anho!*) that the Holy Prophet (*sallallaho alaihe wa sallam!*) got prepared a ring of gold which he used to wear in the right hand. The Companions too, in imitation of him, made rings (of gold); so he threw it away and said; "Now I will never wear this ring".

Note:- Gold was permissible for males in the beginning of Islam, but later on it was prohibited (*haram*), and hence it is illegitimate (*haram*) for menfolks to wear rings of gold.

Necessary Explanation:- If a father or a maternal aunt makes a small child wear a gold ring or gold buttons, it will be illegitimate and they will be guilty.

* * * * * *

XIV

THE DESCRIPTION OF THE HOLY PROPHET'S
(*sallallaho alaihe wa sallam!*)
SWORD

The Holy Prophet (*sallallaho alaihe wa sallam!*) had several swords, each one bearing a proper name. The earliest sword that he had received as an article of inheritance from his father was named Mathoor. The name of one sword was Qazeeb, of another Qala'ee; Tabar and Zulfiqar were also the names of other swords.

Necessary Explanation:- In the world, man, along with fulfilling his needs, should always be prepared to fulfil the demands of faith (*iman*) and Islam; to save and protect his life, property, honour and reputation, he should always keep weapons. If these are kept with the intention of jihad, he would receive recompense for it.

Hadith 1:- It is reported from Hazrat Anas (*razi Allaho anho!*) that the knob of the hilt of the Holy Prophet's (*sallallaho alaihe wa sallam!*) sword was of silver.

Note:- Allamah Baijori has stated that this is the description of the sword named Zulfiqar. This sword was with the Holy Prophet (*sallallaho alaihe wa sallam!*) during the conquest of Mecca.

Necessary Explanation:- It is proved from this hadith that it is permissible to have a silver coating over the hilt of a sword, but gold is not allowed.

Hadith 2:- Ibn Sarin (Allah's mercy be on him!) says; "I made my sword like that of Hazrat Somrah's sword and he used to say that his sword had been made like that of the Holy Prophet's (*sallallaho alaihe wa sallam!*) sword, which was of the make of Banu Hanifa's tribe.

Note:- Banu Hanifa was an Arabian tribe famed as sword makers. The Holy Prophet's (*sallallaho alaihe wa sallam!*) sword was of this tribe's make.

* * * * * *

XV

THE DESCRIPTION OF THE HOLY PROPHET'S
(sallallaho alaihe wa sallam!)
COAT OF MAIL

The Holy Prophet (*sallallaho alaihe wa sallam!*) had seven coats of mail bearing the following proper names:

(1) Zat al-Fuzool, which was so named because of its width. This is the same armour the story of pawning of which with a Jew is famous. (2) Zat al-Hawashi. (3) Zat al-Veshah. (4) Fizza. (5) Sughdiya. (6) Tabra'. (7) Khurnaq.

Hadith:- Hazrat Zubair (*razi Allaho anho!*) reports that in the Battle of Ohad, there were two coats of mail on the Holy Prophet's (*sallallaho alaihe wa sallam!*) body; Zat al-Fuzool and Zat al-Fizza. He wanted to climb a rock which was quite high. But he did not succeed in climbing it because of the heavy weight of two armours and the weakness resulting from the flow of blood from injuries inflicted on his luminous face in this battle. So he made Hazrat Talha (*razi Allaho anho!*) sit down and with his help he succeeded in climbing the rock. Hazrat Zubair (*razi Allaho anho!*) says that he heard the Holy Prophet (*sallallaho alaihe wa sallam!*) saying that "Talha has reserved my intercession for Paradise for himself".

Note:- The Battle of Ohad was very hazardous and frightful, so much so that the Companions thought that he had left the world and had been martyred. It was to set the Companions hearts at rest that he had climbed the rock to show that he was very much alive. Some ulema say that he had climbed the rock to cast a glance at the pagans. Hazrat Talha (*razi Allaho anho!*) had stayed with and assisted the Holy Prophet (*sallallaho alaihe wa sallam!*) most intrepidly, so much so that, after the battle, whenever the Companions recollected its events they used to say that it was Talha's day. Hazrat Talha had made himself a shield for the Holy Prophet (*sallallaho alaihe wa sallam!*) and did not leave him alone although he had received as many as eighty wounds on his own body; morcover, Hazrat Talha had struck the sword so many times and shot so many arrows at the enemy that his hand had become completely tired.

Necessary Explanation:- In having more than one coat of mail the wisdom is that the arms for jihad should be more than necessary, for it is an act of sunnah and the surplus arms can be of use to other mujahids (holy warriors) and thus one can earn recompense. It says in one hadith for more than necessary beds that the extra beds are for Satan. From these two divergent hadiths regarding the surplus things of utility one can understand the spirit of Islam.

Hadith 2:- Hazrat Sa'ib ibn Yazid (*razi Allaho anho!*) reports that on the day of the Battle of Ohad the Holy Prophet (*sallallaho alaihe wa sallam!*), was having two armours on his holy body, wearing one over the other.

Note:- The Holy Prophet's (*sallallaho alaihe wa sallam!*) the armour is not contrary to his trust in Allah (*tawakkul*), because complete trust in Allah, according to the great Sufis, is that one behaves like the common people and conformance to the Shari'ah because one's habit and second nature. Secondly, the Holy Prophet's (*sallallaho alaihe wa sallam!*) behaving like this was for the education of the ummah. Thirdly it is Allah's order; "O ye who believe! Take your precautions (against the infidels; i.e., be vigilant against their stratagem and deceit and also be well-armed while combating them); then advance the proven ones, or advance all together (as the occasion may be)". (IV:71). So, to keep arms and other necessary equipment as per the need of the hour for one's safety is also the order of this verse and who can be more compliant with divine commandments than the Holy Prophet (*sallallaho alaihe wa sallam!*) ?

Necessary Explanation:- Trust in Allah does not mean the giving up of material means; on the contrary, it means that one should trust in Allah after making due provisions. To trust in means and materials is not trust in Allah. Hence the Holy Prophet (*sallallaho alaihe wa sallam!*) took along with him the necessary arms for combat like sword, helmet, armour, etc. but his trust was in Allah alone. Working with his own hands he taught to trust in the Provider of livelihood. (2) Regarding jihad the Divine order in the Quran is to make necessary arrangements as per capacity to overawe your and Allah's enemies.

* * * * * *

XVI

THE HOLY PROPHET'S
(*sallallaho alaihe wa sallam!*)
HELMET

Hadith 1:- Hazrat Anas Razi reports that when the Holy Prophet (*sallallaho alaihe wa sallam!*) entered Mecca on the day of its conquest, there was a helmet on his auspicious head. When he took off the helmet from his head, a man said; "O Apostle of Allah! This Ibn Khatal is grasping the covering of the Ka'ba". The Holy Prophet (*sallallaho alaihe wa sallam!*) said : "Kill him"!

Note:- When the Holy Prophet (*sallallaho alaihe wa sallam!*) had entered Mecca on the day of its conquest, the Meccans were so much struck with terror and confusion that, in their consternation, they could neither find a way to escape nor any place to seek shelter. But the Holy Prophet (*sallallaho alaihe wa sallam!*), due to his innate qualities of affection and mercy, declared : "There is amnesty for those who enter the House of Allah: they must not be killed. There is amnesty for one who remains indoors; and those who enter the houses of such and such leaders of Mecca shall have amnesty".

Notwithstanding this announcement of general amnesty, there were eleven men and six women whose guilt and crimes were unpardonable and so they were made an exception to this general rule and were ordered to be put to death. However, from them also seven men and two women entered the pale of amnesty by becoming Muslims. Of the remaining eight one was Ibn Khatal. He was an early convert to Islam. Once the Holy Prophet (*sallallaho alaihe wà sallam!*) sent him to some place for realising zakat. There he killed his own slave for preparing the meal late. Then he did not return to Madina for the fear that in retaliation (*qisas*) of the said murder he too would be put to death. So he apostatized and went to Mecca. But now, despite his being inside the House of Allah, he was put to death for the said murder.

Necessary Explanation:- Those who boast about democracy and lliberty and blame Islam for encouraging the system of slavery should ponder over this matter. The protection that Islam has afforded the poor and the weak slaves as regards life and property has not been given by any religion and country. Ibn Khatal who was guilty of culpable homicide was well aware of the fact that according to the law of Islam – life for life – he would not escape the penalty of death. And so, having become a renegade, he had taken shelter in Mecca. There he used to satirize the Holy Prophet (*sallallaho alaihe wa sallam!*) and had bought two singing slavemaids who used to please him by the singing verses of his satires. Naturally, such an evil figure, an unrepentant murderer, could not be spared, and so he was ordered to be put to death or was killed by someone. The lives and properties of all non-Muslims, Jews and Christians who happen to live in an Islamic country are as safe and secure as those of the Muslims as long as they remain law-abiding citizens. Is there any other religion which can claim to have the said law in its constitution?

Hadith 2:- It is reported from Hazrat Anas (*Razi Allaho anho!*) that when the Holy Prophet (*sallallaho alaihe wa sallam!*) entered Mecca on the day of its conquest, there was a helmet on his auspicious head. When he took it off, a man asked him about Ibn Khatal

89

and he said that Ibn Khatal was not to be given amnesty and was to be killed.

Note:- Imam Zuhri says that on that day the Holy Prophet (*sallallaho alaihe wa sallam!*) was not in the state of *ahram*. It is proved from this that it is permissible to enter the glorious Mecca without putting on the *ahram;* and this proposition is nearer to Imam Shafi'is belief. But the Hanafite ulema forbid it, because the Holy Prophet (*sallallaho alaihe wa sallam!*) has forbidden to pass through the *Miqat* without the *ahram* and the aforesaid hadith is not a proof for the Hanafites, because, due to the conquest of Mecca, the consecration of Mecca had been lifted on that day, as has been stated in the *Bukhari Sharif*. The Holy Prophet (*sallallaho alaihe wa sallam!*) had said; "it (Mecca) was legitimate for me today; hereafter it will not be legitimate for anyone".

Necessary Explanation:- The Holy Prophet's (*sallallaho alaihe wa sallam!*) meaning was that the consecration of Mecca had been lifted for him on that day so that he could kill by way of punishment anyone inside the *Haram*, but thereafter no one would be permitted or ordered to do so inside the *Haram* as its honour had come back to it till the Day of Doom. It was for this reason that he had entered Mecca without *ahram*, but thereafter it is not permissible for anyone to do so. So, according to the Hanafite opinion, if anyone enters without *ahram*, sacrifice of one 'blood' (a ram or goat) is necessary.

* * * * * *

XVII

THE HOLY PROPHET'S
(sallallaho alaihe wa sallam!)
IMAMAH (Turban)

The length of the Holy Prophet's *(sallallaho alaihe wa sallam!)* Imamah is not mentioned in any one of the famous hadiths. From a tradition in Tibrani, however, it is established that it was seven cubits in length. Allamah Baijori, on Hafiz Ibn Hajar's authority, has reported that this is a baseless tradition. Allamah Zuhri says that he read many books, particularly the biographical ones, but could not find the mention of the length of the Holy Prophet's *(sallallaho alaihe wa sallam!)* turban. It is reported from Imam Nauwavi that the Holy Prophet *(sallallaho alaihe wa sallam!)* had two turbans: one small, of six or seven cubits, and one large, of twelve cubits. The author of Madkhal has stated it to be of only seven cubits.

THE WEARING OF A TURBAN IS A SUNNAH

As stated in the *Fath al-Bari*, even an order for wearing turban has been reported from the Holy Prophet *(sallallaho alaihe wa sallam!)*: "Put on turbans as thereby you will excel in forbearance". Allamah Aiyni has reported that someone had asked Hazrat Abd Allah ibn Umar *(razi Allaho anho!)* if it was a sunnah to wear a turban and he had replied in the affirmative. It says in another hadith; "Wear a turban, for it is a mark of Islam and distinguishes a Muslim from an unbeliever".

Necessary Explanation:- (1) To put on a turban is an act of sunnah; so prayer without putting on a turban is permissible. (2) Even as it is not necessary for the followers in-prayer to wear turbans, it is not necessary for the *imam* too. (3) The prayer will be accomplished without putting on the turban; there will be no discrepancy in the prayer. (4) Since the wearing of the turban is only a sunnah, it is unlawful (*haram*) to compel the imam to wear it. (5) The man who does not meet anyone, does not stir out of house, and does not go as a guest anywhere without wearing a turban, for him it is abominable to say prayers without it.

Hadith 1:- Hazrat Jabir (*razi Allaho anho!*) reports that when the Holy Prophet (*sallallaho alaihe wa sallam!*) entered Mecca on the day of its conquest, there was a black turban on his auspicious head.

Note:- From the previous heading it appears that there was a helmet. But there is no contradiction in it, for he might have worn the turban over the helmet, and in doing so there is no fault. Or, while he was entering there was a helmet on the head and immediately thereafter he might have put on the turban; or he might have put on the helmet over the turban so that the iron might not cause any harm to the head.

Hadith 2:- It is reported from Hazrat Ibn Umar (*razi Allaho anho!*) that whenever the Holy Prophet (*sallallaho alaihe wa sallam!*) put on a turban, he used to keep its end hanging behind between the shoulders. Naf'e says that he had seen Hazrat Abd Allah ibn Umar (*Razi Allaho anho!*) doing like this. Obaidullah, Naf'e's disciple, says that he had seen Hazrat Abu Bakr's (*Razi Allaho anho!*) grandson, Qasim ibn Muhammad, and Hazrat Umar's (*razi Allaho anho!*) grandson, Salim Ibn Abd Allah, doing like this.

Note :- The Holy Prophet's (*sallallaho alaihe wa sallam!*) noble habit was of keeping the tail-end of the turban hanging. Some ulema say that the wearing of the turban without the tail-end hanging is not proven, but researching ulema have stated that it is permissible to wrap the turban without the tail end hanging, and the noble habit was different at different times; sometimes it was kept in the front of the right side and sometime it was kept behind. Allamah Manavi says that both the methods are proven one, but it is better (more correct to keep it one the back between the shoulders).

Hadith 3:- Ibn Abbas (*razi Allaho anho!*) says that once the Holy Prophet (*sallallaho alaihe wa sallam!*) delivered a sermon (khutbah) and there was a black turban or a smooth cloth-band on his head.

Note:- This was the Holy Prophet's (*sallallaho alaihe wa sallam!*) last sermon, delivered during his terminal illness. Thereafter he never ascended the pulpit and never gave any lecture. His head was aching severely while delivering this sermon and hence his having tired a cloth-band around the head is also proven; and his wearing a black turban is also correct because it was already his noble wont.

Amongst the narrators of this hadith there is one whose father's title was Ghasil al-Mala'ika, i.e., one who had been given the last bath by the angels. His story is that when the call for the Battle of Ohad reached his ears, he was busy with his wife. No sooner he heard the noise of the caravan's starting than he accompanied it and did not get so much time that he could have taken a bath. After reaching the battle-field he fell a martyr. Martyrs are not given the last obsequial bath, but the Holy Prophet (*sallallaho alaihe wa sallam!*) saw that angels were bathing him. Hence people began to call him

Ghasil al-Mala'ika. After returning from the holy war, it was inquired from the martyr's wife as to what the matter was that angels gave him a bath. The martyr's widow told the fact. In fact, as it becomes obvious from this true story, it was as easy for the noble Companions to sacrifice their lives for Islam as it is for us to indulge in our worldly desires.

* * * * * *

XVIII

THE DESCRIPTION OF
THE HOLY PROPHET'S
(*sallallaho alaihe wa sallam!*)
'LUNGI'

The Holy Prophet (*sallallaho alaihe wa sallam!*) was habituated to wearing lungi; his wearing pajamas has not been established. Allamah Baijori's ascertainment is also the same. Of course it is proven that he did have a pair of pajamas but it is not proven that he ever wore it. Hafiz Ibn Qayyim's assertion is that the Holy Prophet (*sallallaho alaihe wa sallam!*) had bought a pair of pajamas and this buying was for his wearing. It is inferred from certain hadiths and the Companions also used to wear pajamas with his permission. (*Zad al-Ma'ad*). Abut Omamah (*razi Allaho anho!*) reports that when he told the Holy Prophet (*sallallaho alaihe wa sallam!*) that the scripturaries (Jews and Christians) did put on lungi but not the pajamas, he replied; "Act contrary to them; wear pajamas as well as lungi". Hazrat Abu Huraira (*razi Allaho anho!*) reports in a long hadith that he asked the Holy Prophet (*sallallaho alaihe wa sallam!*) if he wore pajamas and he replied that he did and said; "I have been ordered to cover the *satr*; which other thing does cover the *satr* more than this"? But research scholars have stated this hadith to be 'weak'. (*Nayl al-Awtar*).

The Holy Prophet's (*sallallaho alaihe wa sallam!*) noble habit was to cover his auspicious body with a haick (*chadar*) and to wear a lungi. The haick was four cubits

95

long and two-and-a-half cubits wide. And the lungi was four cubits and one span long and two cubits wide.

Necessary Explanation:- The aforesaid length was necessary for the Holy Prophet's (*sallallaho alaihe wa sallam!*) body. The ummah, however, can keep the length and width as per individual requirements. If one keeps the above-mentioned width and length with the intention of conforming to the sunnah, one will merit recompense.

Hadith 1:- Hazrat Abu Burdah (*razi Allaho anho!*) reports that "Hazrat Ayesha (*razi Allaho anho!*) showed us one patched haick and a coarse lungi, saying that the Holy Prophet (*sallallaho alaihe wa sallam!*) had died in these two clothes".

Note:- The Holy Prophet's (*sallallaho alaihe wa sallam!*) noble habit was to wear such clothes throughout his life. The financial condition (later on) was good but even then he used to put on such clothes. The monetary condition began to improve after the Battle of Khyber and, after the conquest of Mecca, gifts had begun to pour from other states, but notwithstanding these easy circumstances, his life-style, simple and unostentatious, remained unchanged; whatever amount of money or goods that came, he used to expend over others. Imam Nauwavi has stated that these hadiths are a proof of the fact that the Holy Prophet (*sallallaho alaihe wa sallam!*) used to abstain strictly from the worldly comforts. Coarse and thick clothes lead one towards submissiveness and humility, whereas fine, thin and superior-quality clothes create pride, self-conceit, hypocrisy and a desire for publicity and fame in the wearer.

There is a strange story of Maulana Gungohi, the Pride of the Modern Traditionists. When he was circumambulating in a hajj, he saw a blind august man sitting in a corner. Every time, during the circumambulation, the Maulana came near him, the later would say in a low tone; "Wear the pious men's (*saulihin*) clothes – for they are the clothes of the virtuous". Should good clothes come to you, they should be worn. The Holy Prophet (*sallallaho alaihe wa sallam!*), during the major part of his life, used to put on coarse, patched clothes, but if perchance good fine clothes came to him, he would wear them also. He, however, never insisted on wearing fine clothes; he would put on any clothes readily available.

Hadith 2:- Hazrat Obaid bin Khalid (*razi Allaho anho!*) reports; "Once when I was going somewhere in Madina, I heard a man behind me saying; 'Turn your lungi a little up because it keeps you safe from internal as well as external uncleanness, pride etc. (maintaining more cleanliness and saving the cloth from soiling and being rubbed off due to friction against the ground). When I turned my face to look at the speaker of these words, it was the Holy Prophet (*sallallaho alaihe wa sallam!*) himself. So I said; "O Apostle of Allah ! it is a mere coverlet. What pride can one take on it and what is the need of saving it"? He said; "If there is no expediency in it according to you, at least conformance with me still remains there" (i.e., one will merit recompense it one does like that with the intention of conforming with me). After hearing this statement, when I looked at the Holy Prophet's (*sallallaho alaihe wa sallam!*) lungi, it was upto half the calf only".

Note:- Many warnings have been reported regarding lungi and pajamas that cover the ankles; the cloth that hangs below the ankles and the portion of the feet below the ankles, both will be burnt in fire.

Hazrat Abd ar-Rahman (*razi Allaho anho!*) says that when he asked Hazrat Abu Sa'eed Khudri (*Razi Allaho anho!*) a proposition about lungi, he said; "You have asked a knowledgeable man. The Holy Prophet (*sallallaho alaihe wa sallam!*) has said that a Muslim's lungi should be upto half the calf only and it matters little if it is upto the ankles also. But the portion below the ankles on which the lungi will hang will be burned in fire and the man who lets his clothes dangle below out of pride, Allah Most High will not even look at him on the Day of Judgement". (*Abu Da'ud, Muslim*). There are many such warnings in other hadiths too and hence one should pay special attention to this matter; but, unfortunately, quite contrary to this today it has become common to wear lungi or pajamas that reach right below the ankles.

Necessary Explanation:- (1) If the lungi or pajamas reach below the ankles, it is near-prohibited abomination (*makruh-e tahrimi*) to say prayers. (2) There are several disadvantages in wearing lungi or pajamas that reach down below the ankles. (3) the cloth hanging down will be torn. (4) When the cloth is torn and hangs below, the feet may be entangled and one may trip and suffer an injury. (5) One will incur loss in the Hereafter. The Holy Prophet (*sallallaho alaihe wa sallam!*) had said that Allah Most High will not talk with three persons, and will not look at them (mercifully) and will not cleanse them, and for them there is severe torture: (i) One who let his lungi or pajamas hang below the ankles. (ii) One who points out one's obligation. (ii) One who swears falsely. (*Muslim*, part i, p.71).

Hadith 3:- Hazrat Slamah ibn Akw'a (*razi Allaho anho!*) reports that Hazrat Usman Ghani used to keep his lungi upto the middle of the calves and used to say that "the condition of the lungi of my chief, the Holy Prophet (*sallallaho alaihe wa sallam!*), was like this only".

Hadith 4:- Hazrat Huzalfa ibn Yaman (*Razi Allaho anho!*) reports that "the Holy Prophet (*sallallaho alaihe wa sallam!*), grasping the flesh of my calf or his own, said that this is the limit for the lungi; if you are not content with this, let it be a little lower, but if you are not content even with this, let it be a little lower, but if you are not content with this then the lungi has no right over the ankles and hence it must not reach the ankles."

Necessary Explanation:- The Holy Prophet (*sallallaho alaihe wa sallam!*) placed his hand on the calf to point out the limit of the lungi. Alas! the ummah has forsaken this instruction. (2) The said order is meant for menfolks. (3) For the womenfolk it is proper (*ja'iz*) to let the pajamas dangle below, from more than a span to a cubit, but how ironical, that the women's pajamas have become high and the men's have gone low, and thus both the sexes are guilty of committing prohibited act.. (4) If part of a woman's calf becomes naked, her prayer will be vitiated (*fasid*).

* * * * * * *

XIX

THE HOLY PROPHET'S
(sallallaho alaihe wa sallam!)
GAIT

The Holy Prophet's *(sallallaho alaihe wa sallam!)* gait has already been referred to in the description of his noble features, but some more details are given here.

Hadith 1:- Abu Huraira *(razi Allaho anho!)* reports; "I have not seen anyone more handsome than the Holy Prophet *(sallallaho alaihe wa sallam!)* his lustre and radiance was such as if the sun itself shone in his face. And I did not see anyone who walked more briskly than him; it seemed as if the earth itself was being rolled up for him, for if he was here this moment, he would be there in a crack. Though he used to walk with his normal gait, we could keep pace with him with difficulty; that is, we had to walk more briskly with him".

Hadith 2:- Ibrahim ibn Muhammad reports that whenever Hazrat Ali *(razi Allaho anho!)* described the Holy Prophet *(sallallaho alaihe wa sallam!)*, while walking, used to put his noble steps firmly and vigorously; he did not drag along like women. From his brisk and vigorous gait it appeared as if he was descending from a high place.

Necessary Explanation:- The prophets' miracle *(mujizah)* is the saints' *(awlia's)* miraculous act *(karamah)*, which, in Arabic, is called *Tai al-arz;* i.e., the earth is rolled up. So even when the Holy Prophet *(sallallaho alaihe wa sallam!)* walked normally, the

Companions used to find it difficult to keep pace with him. (The reader is requested to read again the prophetic manner of walking described in the foregone).

* * * * * * *

XX

THE DESCRIPTION OF THE HOLY PROPHET'S
(sallallaho alaihe wa sallam!)
QIN'A (KERCHIEF)

Note:- *Qin'a* is that piece of cloth which the Holy Prophet *(sallallaho alaihe wa sallam!)* used to keep under his turban so as to save the latter from being stained from hair-oil. Besides this, the ulema have described other advantages also.

Necessary Explanation:- Some ulema have given it the heading "Taqqan'o". That is, the Holy Prophet *(sallallaho alaihe wa sallam!)* used to keep a kerchief over his head in order to protect the face from heat and cold. So, when he went to inform Hazrat Abu Bakr Siddiq *(razi Allaho anho!)* about *Hijrat* (migration), he had put a cloth upon his auspicious turban to protect himself from the scorching heat.

Hadith 1:- Hazrat Anas *(razi Allaho anho!)* reports that the Holy Prophet *(sallallaho alaihe wa sallam!)* used to keep a kerchief on his head. Having become oily, it looked like the cloth of an oil-presser.

Note:- Though this kerchief, having soaked oil from the hair looked like the oily clothes of an oil-presser, it was a prophetic peculiarity that the kerchief did not become dirty or soiled, and neither lice could infest his clothes nor bed-bugs could suck his blood. And Allamah has reported it from Manavi that flies too could not sit upon his holy body.

Explanation:- Allah Most High had protected the holy being of the Holy Prophet (*sallallaho alaihe wa sallam!*) from such harmful things.

* * * * * * *

XXI

DESCRIPTION OF THE HOLY PROPHET'S *(sallallaho alaihe wa sallam!)* MANNER OF SITTING

Hadith 1:- Hazrat Qailah *(razi Allaho anha!)* reports that "I saw the Holy Prophet *(sallallaho alaihe wa sallam!)* squatting in the mosque (with such an humble expression) that I began to tremble due to his awe".

Note:- The ulema are divided as regards the squatting posture. This posture, as is well-known, consists in sitting on one's bottom, while the knees are kept raised and encircled by the arms. The cause of awesomeness was that it appeared to be a condition of worry and anxiety and the Holy Prophet *(sallallaho alaihe wa sallam!)* could not feel worried and anxious due to any ordinary reason. So she inferred that perhaps some punishment was imminent for the ummah, for whom the Holy Prophet *(sallallaho alaihe wa sallam!)* was always anxious and concerned. It is also mentioned in this hadith that, seeing her consternation, one of the Companions told him that poor woman was feeling confounded. "I was", says Hazrat Qailah, "just behind paying any attention towards me, he simply said; "O poor woman! Be at peace"! No sooner he uttered these words than all my fear and terror vanished".

Necessary Explanation:- It was a divine light in the form of a miracle that anyone who came to the Holy Prophet *(sallallaho alaihe wa sallam!)* for the first time used to be overawed on seeing him.

Hadith 2:- Abbad's uncle, Abd Allah bin Zaid (*razi Allaho anho!*) reports that he saw the Holy Prophet (*sallallaho alaihe wa sallam!*) lying flat on his back in the mosque, keeping one leg over the other.

Note:- In the tradition recorded in the *Muslim Sharif*, such posture of lying down is forbidden. The ulema have explained both the hadiths separately. What is clear is that there are two manners of sleeping like this and both are correct. As described in the above-mentioned hadith, the first manner is to place one leg over the other while sleeping and it is permissible. In the other one knee is kept raised and the other leg is placed over it, and this is impermissible, as is well-known from the tradition in the *Muslim Sharif*. The reason for its being impermissible is that there was the custom of wearing lungi in Arabia and in this manner of lying there is always the possibility of the *satr* getting bare.

From this hadith arises another question: What has this hadith to do with the manner of sitting? The answer is that in this chapter the word 'sitting' has been used in a wider sense, which includes both sitting and lying down. According to Hafiz Ibn Hajar, if this manner of lying down in the mosque is proper (*ja'iz*), then sitting in either manner is all the more proper.

Necessary Explanation:- (1) It is necessary for every man and woman to be careful about *satr* while sitting down or standing up. (2) Due to drowsiness and fatigue caused by devotions, it is permissible to sleep in the mosque. (3) One should adopt the posture of humility and slavehood (*'abadiyat*) while sitting and save oneself from the manner of pride and arrogance.

Hadith 3:- It is reported from Hazrat Abu Sa'eed Khudri (*razi Allaho anho!*) that whenever the Holy

105

Prophet (sallallaho alaihe wa sallam!) sat in the mosque he used to sit with knees raised, encircled by his arms.

Note:- This manner of sitting is a posture of humility and it was for this reason that the Holy Prophet (*sallallaho alaihe wa sallam!*) and the noble Companions (*razi Allaho anho!*) used to sit like this very often. It, however, does not mean that he always used to sit like this. So now there remains no contradiction with the tradition of the *Abu Da'ud Sharif* in which it is stated that the Holy Prophet (*sallallaho alaihe wa sallam!*) used to squat in the mosque after the Fajr prayer till sunrise.

There is also comfort in sitting on one's bottom with raised knees. It is said in one hadith that to sit on one's bottom is the Arab's wall for there are no walls in deserts for reclining against. Hence to sit like this was to sit reclining. At times the knees are wrapped with a chadar or a handkerchief instead of encircling them with arms.

Necessary Explanation:- To adopt the said posture in sitting is proper provided one has put on a lungi or pajamas, but it is not proper if one is wearing only a chadar, because if it falls off in sleep, the *satr* will be bared. (2) To sit in the said manner awaiting for the prayer is forbidden, because if one falls asleep, the ablution will become invalid.(3) To sit like this for the Friday and the old prayers is also forbidden.

* * * * * * *

XXII

THE DESCRIPTION OF THE HOLY PROPHET'S
(*Sallallaho alaihe wa sallam!*)
PILLOW

Hadith 1:- Hazrat Jabir ibn Somrah (*razi Allaho anho!*), reports that he saw the Holy Prophet (*Sallallaho alaihe wa sallam!*) reclining against a pillow which was lying on his left side.

Note:- It is proper to put the pillow both on the left and the right sides. The word 'left' in the hadith is not due to any particular reason. It is a mere accident, for in other hadiths the words 'left side' are not mentioned.

Hadith 2:- It is reported from Hazrat Abu Johaifa (*razi Allaho anho!*) that the Holy Prophet (*sallallaho alaihe wa sallam!*) said : "I do not take my meals reclining my back against anything".

Note:- To sit reclining for eating is contrary to humility and, besides one eats more like this. Some ulema assert that by eating like this the stomach is enlarged and the food is not digested quickly. The Holy Prophet (*sallallaho alaihe wa sallam!*) stated his own habit so that others may conform to it.

There are four ways of reclining; (1) Either the left or the right side is reclined against a wall or a pillow (2) The palm may be placed on the ground; (3) One may squat upon a cushion or a bed. (4) The back may be reclined against a pillow or a wall. All these four manners are included in reclining for eating.

Necessary Explanation:- Hence all these four manners of reclining while eating must be avoided. More details may be seen under the heading 'Manner of Eating'.

A portion of a long hadith related by Hazrat Abu Bakr (*razi Allaho anho!*):- The Holy Prophet (*sallallaho alaihe wa sallam!*), reclining against something, was saying: "Shall I not tell you the grave sins"? The Companions said: "Why not? Please do tell us". Then he said: "To make anyone a partner of Allah in His Being and Attributes; and to disobey parents". Then he gave up the support, sat up and said: "To give false evidence (to perjure) and to utter a falsehood". These words he was repeating again and again.'

'Marking the strain', say the Companions, 'he was feeling in speaking these words repeatedly, we wished he would better become quiet.

Necessary Explanation:- (1) It is established from the said hadith that reclining against anything while **remembering Allah, reading the holy Quran, imparting** knowledge or teaching students in not contrary to perfect decorum. The rights of those present in an assembly (majlis) are not disregarded by one's reclining. (*Mawahib*, p. 79). A religious teacher is also a human being, particularly one who is busy in *zikr* and then in teaching since the early dawn; if he sits reclining against a pillow in the seminary, it is quite right and proper (*ja'iz*). The foolish and the ignorant consider it an incivility, but they should know that it is not contrary to the prophetic civility. They must not compare ours with

108

the European culture and etiquette. How can the rightdown worldlings who are habituated to rise up from their beds at 8.00 in the morning understand? They would do well to know the prophetic decorum and hold their carping tongues.

(2) It is proper (*ja'iz*) to recline against something in a majlis. (*Umdat al-Qari Sharh-e Bukhari*, vol.ii, p.22: Kirmani's *Sharh-e Bukhari*, vol.ii, p. 18; *Fathal-Bari Sharh-e Bukhari*, vol.i, p. 159)

* * ** * * *

XXIII

THE HOLY PROPHET'S
(*Sallallaho alaihe wa sallam!*)
RECLINING AGAINST THINGS
OTHER THAN A PILLOW

The Holy Prophet (*sallallaho alaihe wa sallam!*), besides reclining against a pillow, as described in the preceding chapter, also used to take support of others, particularly during illness.

Hadith 1:- Hazrat Anas (*razi Allaho anho!*) reports that the Holy Prophet (*sallallaho alaihe wa sallam!*) was ill. So, supporting himself on Hazrat Osamah, he came out of the house and led the Companions in prayer. A Yemenite chadar was upon his holy body.

Hadith 2:- Hazrat Fazl ibn Abbas (*razi Allaho anho!*) reports that he went to the Holy Prophet (*sallallaho alaihe wa sallam!*) during his fatal illness. At that time a yellow band on cloth was tied around his head. He said: "O Fazl! Tie this band tightly": Obeying the order, Fazl tied it tightly. "Then", says Fazl, "he sat up and thereafter, supporting himself upon me, he came to there mosque".

Note:- It is a lengthy hadith. The Holy Prophet (*sallallaho alaihe wa sallam!*) came to the mosque and asked Fazl to gather the people. Fazl complied with the behest and when the people had gathered there, the Holy Prophet (*sallallaho alaihe wa sallam!*) said: "My time of departing from you has drawn near. So, if I may have slapped anyone on the waist, here is my waist. Retaliate If I may have attacked the honour of anyone, let him attack mine. If I have had anyone's money on me (i.e., if I owe money to any one), let him demand it from me. Let no one think that I would be angry at such a demand; it's not my nature to bear malice and it is also far below the dignity of a prophet to do so. Know it well that the man who demands the fulfillment of his right from me is very much dear to me; or let him forgo it and forgive me so that I may go cheerfully before Allah. I will not be content with this proclamation; I will repeat it again". After the Zuhr prayer he proclaimed again and also observed: "If any one has a right to discharge, let him discharge it without thinking of the worldly disgrace, for the worldly disgrace and ignominy is far less than that of the Hereafter".

A Companion got up and said: "You owe me three dirhems". The Holy Prophet (sallallaho alaihe wa sallam!) got it paid and declared that if any one wished him to pray for him, he could do so. Two men got up and, expressing contrition for being hypocrites and liars, forswore these evil morals and requested him to pray for them. He prayed for them. Then he went to Hazrat Ayesha's (razi Allaho anha!) room and there also he made a similar proclamation as he had done among the menfolk.

The Companions' confession of hypocrisy was due to Allah's fear, which was so intense in them that they used to consider their own actions insignificant. It is reported in one hadith that another Companion got up and, confessing his own timidity, requested the Holy Prophet (sallallaho alaihe wa sallam!) to pray for him. He prayed and Hazrat Fazl reports that "after the prophetic invocation we used to mark that there was none more

111

intrepid than that Companion". Hazrat Umar (*razi Allaho anho!*) said something to the gathering at which the Holy Prophet (*sallallaho alaihe wa sallam!*) said: "Umar is with me and I am with Umar - wherever he may go".

Necessary Explanation:- Every man should try to discharge the right of all and sundry in order to save himself from the ignominy and disgrace of the Hereafter.

* * * * * * *

XXIV

THE HOLY PROPHET'S
(*Sallallaho alaihe wa sallam!*)
MANNER OF EATING

Hadith 1:- Hazrat Ka'b ibn Malik (*razi Allaho anho!*) reports that the Holy Prophet (*sallallaho alaihe wa sallam!*) used to lick his fingers thrice (after finishing the meal).

Note:- After having taken the meal, it is praiseworthy (*mustahab*) to lick the fingers before washing the hands. According to some ulema, the licking of the fingers thrice, as said in the above-mentioned hadith, is praiseworthy as the fingers thus will be cleaned fully.

Mulla Ali Qari's assertion is that the purpose is not to lick the fingers thrice but it is to lick the three fingers, as it appears from another tradition. But the opinion of some ulema is that to lick thrice and lick three fingers both are praiseworthy severally.

Necessary Explanation:- To eat with one finger is the Satan's manner; it is stated in the *Ihya al-Ulum* that Allah becomes angry with one who eats with one finger only. To eat with two fingers is an act of sunnah; it is the manner of the prophets. And to eat with four or five fingers is the sign of the greedy and a habit of the esurient.

Hadith 2:- Hazrat Ka'b ibn Malik (*razi Allaho anho!*) reports that the Holy Prophet's (*sallallaho alaihe wa sallam!*) habit was to eat with three fingers, which also used to lick after having finished the meal.

Note:- It says in certain traditions that he used to lick first the middle finger, then the index finger and then the thumb. In licking in this order there are different expediencies: firstly, the process of licking may proceed towards the right side, and also because the middle finger being longer is besmeared more, it should be licked clean first.

Allamah Khattabi has stated that some ignorant, foolish fellows consider it had to lick the fingers. But what is bad in it? The same food that was being eaten is sticking to the fingers. What ill is there in licking the same food?

Ibn Hajar has stated that if a man considers his own act to be bad, it is arguable, but if some unthinking fellow considers the prophetic act to be bad, there is fear of his (objector's) infidelity (*kufr*).

As a matter of fact, there is a great role of personal habits in such matters. When Maulana Zakariya Sahib (may his greatness last long!) went to Hejaz, some Hejazi friends who had never visited India inquired from him about the fruit that grows in India and is called 'mango', which is taken into the mouth and sucked again and again (till all the juice has been sucked up). They asked this question with such a feeling of abomination and nausea as if they would soon vomit. But no Indian considers it so nauseous and sucks it with great relish and eagerness. Similarly, the spoon with which *firni* (a sort of pudding made with ground rice and milk) is eaten

114

is taken fully into the mouth and then the same spoon is dipped again and again into the plate of *firni* for eating. Such examples are many. When a man is habituated to eating like this, he does not have the slightest doubt of its being abominable. The thought of its being abominable crosses the mind only because we have given up the sunnah habit of licking the fingers, and hence this act of sunnah must not be given up.

Necessary Explanation:- Since food is a bounty from Allah, any trace of it left on the fingers after eating must be valued. The Holy Prophet's (*sallallaho alaihe wa sallam!*) habit was to eat with three fingers, but it is permissible, as per necessity, to use all the five fingers for eating. Obviously, one will make small morsels if one uses only three fingers. Mullah Ali Qari writes that to eat with all the five fingers is the sign of the esurient. If a morsel is large, there is also fear of its getting stuck up in the throat, and even if it is swallowed somehow, it will be a burden on the stomach. However, if the food is soft and thin, it is permitted to use all the five fingers. To eat with three fingers (the middle finger, the index finger and the thumb) is praiseworthy.

Hadith 3:- It is reported from Hazrat Anas (*razi Allaho anho!*) that dates were brought before the Holy Prophet (*sallallaho alaihe wa sallam!*) and he was eating them; the hunger was so acute that he could not sit by himself but had to take support from something to squatting.

Note:- That is, he was reclining against the wall or some other thing. To recline while eating is forbidden by hadiths but since here there is the excuse of weakness, neither this tradition can be deemed to be contradictory to those hadiths that forbid reclining nor can one prove

115

from it the praiseworthiness of eating reclining without an excuse.

Necessary Explanation:- (1) If the Islamic Shari'ah is studied thoroughly, it can be realised that Islam has taken care of every human aspect and condition. While the sunnah and praiseworthy (*mustahab*) methods for the healthy are different, it is permissible for the sick to take support upon or recline against something for eating.

(2) Bread should be eaten with the help of three fingers, and rice too – if it be possible. If need be, the use of all the five fingers is also permissible. To partake food sitting, it is permitted to eat standing. It is in this sense that Islam is easy, for every one, the rich and the poor, the sick and the healthy, has been commanded in accordance to one's capacity.

(3) It is proved from the licking of the fingers that one should take food with one's hands. The Holy Prophet (*sallallaho alaihe wa sallam!*) did not use spoon for eating, and hence our predecessors (salaf) used to avoid spoons.

It is stated in the *Kashshaf* that once when different dishes were arranged on Harun al-Rashid's dinner-cloth and spoons were also put on it, Imam Abu Yusuf, who was present there, said to the caliph: "Your grandfather, Hazrat Ibn Abbas (*razi Allaho anho!*), in interpretation of the verse "*laqad karrama Bani Adama*", has said: 'we have made fingers for the sons of man wherewith they eat'. Harun, hearing this, immediately returned the spoons and ate with his fingers.

116

(4) The ulema, realising their responsibility, should acquit themselves of it on suitable occasions and thus discharge the obligation of preaching.

Unfortunately, the Muslims of the period, instead of reviving the prophetic sunnahs, are taking on European habits and customs and are using spoon, fork and knife. The Europeanised Muslims consider it an advancement but they do not realise that by giving up the prophetic sunnahs they are only causing weakness to their faith (*iman*).

* * * * * * *

XXV

THE DESCRIPTION OF THE HOLY PROPHET'S
(*sallallaho alaihe wa sallam!*)
BREAD

(What kind of bread and how much he used to eat?)

Hadith 1:- Hazrat Ayesha (*razi Allaho anha!*) reports that till the Holy Prophet's (*sallallaho alaihe wa sallam!*) death the members of his household did not eat even barley-bread to their fill even for two days consecutively.

Note:- That is, although they might have eaten dates to their fill often, it never happened till his demise that they might have received barley-bread in sufficient quantity even for two days on a stretch to fill their bellies.

But here arises the question that since the Holy Prophet (*sallallaho alaihe wa sallam!*) used to give one year's expenses at a time to each one of his holy wives (a fact proven from hadiths), there is apparently a contradiction between this hadith and the hadiths that describe the annual expenses.,

The ulema have explained this seeming contradiction in different ways. One of these explanations is that the word "*ahl*" ("members of the household") in this hadith is extra and by it is meant the person of the Holy Prophet (*sallallaho alaihe wa*

118

sallam!), himself. Let alone a whole year, stocking provisions for himself even for a day is not proven.

One explanation is that the Holy Prophet (*sallallaho alaihe wa sallam!*), did allot the yearly expenses but the holy wives themselves, in their eagerness for earning recompense, used to spend from their share in alms and charity.

Hadith 2:- Hazrat Abu Ommah (*razi Allaho anho!*) reports that barley-bread was not left over in the Holy Prophet's (*sallallaho alaihe wa sallam!*) house.

Note:- Even if sometimes barley-bread was prepared in the house, it used to be not in so much quantity that it could be left over, for it used to be insufficient even for eating to their fill. Besides, there used to be numerous guests often in addition to the Companions of the Suffa who were his permanent guests. And hence there could be no question of left-overs from the barley-bread.

Hadith 3:- Hazrat Ibn Abbas (*razi Allaho anho!*) reports that the Holy Prophet (*sallallaho alaihe wa sallam!*) and the members of his household used to pass night after night at a stretch without food, for there used to be nothing for eating at night, and frequently his food consisted of barley-bread (though sometimes bread of wheat was also afforded).

Note:- There were several well-to-do and affluent persons among the Companions but the Holy Prophet (*sallallaho alaihe wa sallam!*) and the members of the household would not let anyone know their condition.

Necessary Explanation:- (1) The said poverty and straitened circumstances had been adopted by him

119

voluntarily, otherwise Allah Most High had told him that "if you wish, I will transmute the Mount Ohad into gold", and he had replied: "I like my present condition that sometimes I may eat and sometimes remain hungry". The holy wives, too, in conformance with their holy husband, used to observe patience and remain contented with their lot, never giving any clue to anyone that they were often starving. Had the Companions come to know of such circumstance, they would have surely inundated and supplied the holy family with gifts and presents, but the members of the household were so content, so serene and patient that they never gave even the slightest hint about their plight.

(2) In poor circumstances one should save oneself from begging.

Hadith 4:- Someone asked Hazrat Sahi ibn Sa'd (*razi Allaho anho!*): "Has the Holy Prophet (*sallallaho alaihe wa sallam!*) ever eaten bread of finely-ground white flour"? He replied: "Finely-ground flour must never have come before him till the last phase of his life". Then the enquirer asked: "Did you people have sieves during his time"? "no", replied he. "How did you then bake the barley-bread". inquired the enquirer. "We", replied Sahl "used to puff at the barley-flour so that the thick straws and chaff were blown off and the remaining flour was kneaded".

Note:- *Allahus-Samad!* Today it is considered difficult to eat wheat-bread of unsifted flour, although bread prepared from unsifted flour is easily digested whereas the bread of finely-ground flour (*maida*) is heavy. Even so, by dint of affluence this extravagant custom has become prevalent in many families. Some ulema have stated that the first innovation (*bid'ah*) that

120

entered Islam is the use of sieves. It does not mean, however, that it is reckoned to be that sort of innovation which is considered contrary to the sunnah; it has been called an innovation only because it was a new practice, as otherwise there is no question regarding its being permissible.

Necessary Explanation:- (1) Hakims and doctors also advise people to avoid eating bread of finely-ground flour (maida). (2) The custom of eating bread smeared with ghee or oil, in also harmful. (3) To sift flour with a sieve is permissible. (4) The sunnah method is to use unsifted flour. (5) Innovation means a 'new custom' because sieves were not in use during the prophetic times, (6) To eat soft chapatis (round, flat and thin bread) is permissible. (7) To cut bread with a knife or pen-knife is against civility (adab)

Hadith 5:- Hazrat Anas (razi Allaho anho!) reports that the Holy Prophet (sallallaho alaihe wa sallam!) never took his meals on a table nor in small plates. Chapatis were never prepared for him. Anas says that he asked Qatadah as to where then he used to keep his food for eating. "This very piece of leather which was used as a dinner-cloth", replied Qatadah.

Note:- Allamah Manavi and Mullah Ali Qari have stated that to eat on a table has always been the habit of the proud people. It is stated in the Kaukab al-Durri that since in our own times eating on a dining-table creates resemblance with the Christians, it is a near-prohibited abomination (makruh-e tahrimi). The problem of resemblance is extremely important. Warnings have been given against it in various manners in numerous hadiths. In eating, drinking and clothing, so much so that even in devotions, we have been prevented

121

from adopting resemblance with the non-Muslims; as such, the Holy Prophet (*sallallaho alaihe wa sallam!*) has commanded to add one more fast to the fast of Ashura (16th of Muharram), either before or after it, so as to avoid resemblance with the Jews.

Necessary Explanation:- The prophetic warning is that the people who adopt resemblance with other communities belong to them; that is, on the Day of Resurrection they will be resurrected with them. It is a very serious matter and hence one should be very much concerned and fearful about it. In the present times the wealthy Muslims who have been so much impressed by the Jewish and Christian customs and manners that they approve of every European style and like to have dining-table, chairs, forks, knives and spoons for eating, should take a lesson and warning from a factual incident mentioned in the *Tazkirat al-Rashid* as follows:-

During the British regime in India, an English district collector embraced Islam at the hands of a moulvi and began to study the Islamic beliefs and the holy Quran under his instruction and guidance. When he was transferred to another district, the said moulvi introduced him to another moulvi of that place for receiving religious education. After sometime when the Englishman became sure that he would be paying the debt of nature before long, he gave a sum of money to his new instructor and told him: "My countrymen will bury me in the Christian cemetry. So take this money. When they have buried me there, you come there with our Muslim brethren, take out my corpse and bury it in the Muslim graveyard" The said moulvi, sometime after the English neo-Muslim's obsequies, went to the Englishmen's graveyard alone, dug the grave and opened the coffin to take out the body. But what did he see there? He was astounded to see that instead of the neophyte's corpse there was lying the dead body of that moulvi at whose hands the Englishman had accepted Islam. This mysterious transfer of the dead body from the Muslim graveyard to the Christian cemetery and vice versa was most probably due to the likings of the two men. The Muslim moulvi used to appreciate the English people's lifestyle before his own friends while the English neo-Muslim liked the Islamic method of obsequies.

Another story : A dream is not a proof but it can surely provide a warning. About fifteen years ago a student reading in the fifth Arabic class at Jami'a Islamiyya, Dabhel (Dist. Surat, Gujarat, India) saw in a dream that he was wearing an English hat. He asked its interpretation from me (this writer), but I advised him to write to Shaikh al-Hadith Maulana Zakariya Sahib. The Shaikh replied the said student was fond of some English custom or style and the boy did confess that he was fond of the English language.

So the Muslims should ponder over their present-day condition. The Companions (*razi Allaho anhum!*) asked the Holy Prophet (*sallallaho alaihe wa sallam!*) 'O Apostle of Allah! You will be on a very high rank in Paradise whereas we will be left much below. What will we do then without you"? "Every man," replied he, "will rise up on the Day of Judgement along with those people whose manners and customs he had liked". Hearing this reply, the Companions were very much pleased.

Hence cherish love for and act according to the Holy Prophet's (*sallallaho alaihe wa sallam!*) sunnahs if you wish to rise up on the Day of Judgement along with and be in the company of the prophets, Siddiqs (the sincere

123

ones), martyrs, and the virtuous. Your love for and acting upon the sunnahs will make both your religious and worldly lives successful; so take pains and endeavour hard. Give up eating on the dining-table and also the use of fork and spoon. Use your fingers which are a divine gift and thank Allah profusely for this bounty.

XXVI

REGARDING THE CHAIR

The sunnah practice consists in sitting on the floor for eating. The use of dining-table and chairs is the practice of the Jews and the Christians and hence a near-prohibited abomination (*makruh*-e Tahrimi).

So, the functionaries of the seminaries - those religious schools where the deputy caliphs of the Holy Prophet (*sallallaho alaihe wa sallam!*) are in the making i.e., receiving education and training - should realise their responsibility. When these students are provided tables and chairs for dining in contrast to the sunnah practice, how will they revive the sunnahs when they go back to their native-places after completing the education? Hence this practice should be renounced, for, once they are habituated to taking their meals on tables it will be difficult for them to sit on the floor for dining.

(2) The Holy Prophet (*sallallaho alaihe wa sallam!*) never took his meals in small plates: on the contrary, he used to sit with ten, fifteen people around a large tray and eat from it. To east separately is also one of the signs of pride; those who adopt this practice surely nurse a sneaking hatred for the poor and an aversion for those who dine jointly from the same tray.

The other meaning of eating from large tray is that there used to be no chutney or pickles in small dishes; on the contrary, their food used to be simple and was served in large trays.

(3) Though the people today sit together for dining but the separatism can be witnessed at the same dinner-table, for each dinner takes out food in his own small plate for eating. Even if they sit on the floor around a dinner-cloth, they eat separately. How can then there be love and unity among them? How can they become one people?

(4) There can be only fried and gravyless foods in small plates, whereas large plates or trays can contain a lot of soup or gravy, it was for this reason that the Holy Prophet (*sallallaho alaihe wa sallam!*) said: "Add water and prepare more gravy and keep taking care of your neighbour." And it was because of this thoughtfulness and fellow-feeling that the Holy Prophet (*sallallaho alaihe wa sallam!*) never ate from small plates.

(5) The Holy Prophet (*sallallaho alaihe wa sallam!*) never ate soft chapatis - a necessary part of the fare of the well-to-do and the luxurious people. Even today the hard workers and labourers eat hard, thick bread; the Holy Prophet (*sallallaho alaihe wa sallam!*) too usually barley-bread. This is the reason that august men advise, orally as well as in writing, and I have heard it several times, particularly from Shaikh al-Hadith Maulana Zakariya Sahib, that we should study the Holy Prophet's (*sallallaho alaihe wa sallam!*) biography especially the *Shama'il-e Tirmizi*, and try to act upon it, as far as possible, and introduce the prophetic methods of eating into our lives.

Hazrat Ayesha (*razi Allaho anha!*) used to say: "The first ever innovation that came into Islam was 'eating to one's fill.' Good soft food and fried things induce man to eat to satiation, whereas coarse, unrefined food is eaten

126

as per necessity only and man is saved from many ailments. May Allah bestow upon us the grace to act upon the said acts of sunnah! Amen!

Hadith 6:- Masruq (*razi Allaho anho!*) reports that he went to Hazrat Ayesha (*razi Allaho anha!*). She sent for some food for him and began to say: "I never eat to my fill but when I feel like weeping, I begin to weep." Masruq asked her why she felt like weeping. She said: "That condition of the Holy Prophet (*sallallaho alaihe wa sallam!*) in which he departed from us comes to my mind that it never happened that he might have eaten mutton or bread to his fill twice in a single day."

Hadith 7:- It is reported from Hazrat Anas (*razi Allaho anho!*) that the Holy Prophet (*sallallaho alaihe wa sallam!*) never ate on a table nor ever chapatis.

Note:- The Holy Prophet (*ṣallallaho alaihe wa sallam!*) preferred to live in poverty (*faqr*). But as regards this, there are two statements of the ulema. One is that he had himself chosen poverty voluntarily and hence he used to get less; the other is that he used to get ample wealth and food, but much of these he used to give away in alms and charity.

Explanation:- Poverty was adopted by him of his own volition and choice, otherwise Allah Most High had offered to transmute Mount Ohad into gold for him.

* * * * * * *

XXVII

SOME MORE DETAILS REGARDING EATING FROM THE BUKHARI SHARIF AND ITS COMMENTARIES

Hazrat Abu Huraira (*razi Allaho anho!*) reports that the Holy Prophet (*sallallaho alaihe wa sallam!*) never ate to his fill consecutive for three days. (*Bukhari*, vol. ii, p.809). It is stated in the *Tirmizi* and the *Muslim* that even barley-bread he did not eat to his fill consecutively for three days.

Necessary Explanation:- It is the opinion of certain ulema that he would not assuage his hunger for want of food but research scholars say that there were certain reasons for his not eating to his fill.

(1) Whatever he received, he used to give it away to the poor and the needy. (2) To sate the hunger fully is a bad thing. Fuzayl ibn Iyaz (Allah's mercy be on him!) says that to eat to satiety is bad and harmful, Imam Shafi'i (Allah's mercy be on him!) observes that hunger cleanses the heart. Hazrat Hozaife (*razi Allaho anho!*) reports that the man who eats less, his stomach remains healthy and heart clean, whereas the man who gorges to his fill, his stomach gets upset and heart becomes hard. One tradition says: "Don't kill your heart by indulging in excessive eating and drinking, for the heart is a fruit and even as a cultivated field is spoiled by excessive watering, the heart, too, is spoiled by surfiet of food and drink."

Hazrat Ma'di Karab (*razi Allaho anho!*) reports that only that much food is sufficient for man whereby his back may remain straight. (*Umat at-Qari,* vol.xxi, p.27)

*****

XXVIII

REGARDING THE APPEASING OF APPETITE

Imam Bukhari (Allah's mercy be on him!), in his book (vol.ii, p. 810), has recorded three hadiths under the heading: The Assuaging of the Appetite.

Allamah Aiyni (Allah's mercy be on him!) writes in his book (vol.xxi, p. 33) that wherever the words "eating to his fill" have come, they mean: (1) By eating some dates, mutton and bread the hunger was assuaged but the stomach was not full. (2) Ibn Battal (Allah's mercy be on him!) writes that the Holy Prophet (*sallallaho alaihe wa sallam!*) sometimes ate to his fill to show that it was permissible to do so, but it is not better to eat to satiety, because he has also said that the man who satiates himself in the world will be hungry in the Hereafter. Tabri (Allah's mercy be on him!) writes that there is a limit to eating to one's fill; to glut more than that comes under extravagance. (*Umdat al-Qary*, vol. xxi. p. 33). To indulge the appetite so much that the stomach may be overloaded, body may become heavy and overeating which may cause indisposition and illness, is prohibited (*haram*).

When is it called hunger? In the present age as soon as the fixed time for eating comes, people sit down at the dinner-cloth. But this is not hunger; it is false hunger. One should save oneself from appeasing it.

What is called hunger? Allamah Badr al-Din Aiyni has stated two signs of hunger:-

(1) One may start eating bread only, without waiting for the curry. (2) If the saliva is cast on the floor and the house-fly does not sit upon it, it will be called true hunger (vol.xxi, p. 33).

Imam Ghazali (Allah's mercy be on him!) writes in his *Ihya al-Ulum* that, having written seven times, he has written about order, permission, abomination and unlawfulness. Act upon them and protect your health. You will be able to appreciate the value of religion by these, as the human physical needs have been outlined in them. Those seven items are as follows:-

(1) To eat only that much that may sustain life. (2) Being alive one may discharge the obligations of prayer and fasting. To appease hunger to be able to discharge both these duties is indispensable (*wajib*). (3) One may acquire strength by eating so as to say supererogatory (*nafl*) prayers. (4) By eating one may have the necessary strength to work and earn money; to each this much is praiseworthy (*mustahab*). (5) To eat to fill one-third part of the stomach is permissible. (6) To eat so much that the stomach may become heavy and one may feel sleepy is abominable (*makruh*), (7) To eat so much as to cause indisposition is prohibited (*haram*).

XXIX

THE CAUSE OF EVERY DISEASE

The Holy Prophet's (sallallaho alaihe wa sallum!) statement is that the root-cause of disease is to eat over a full stomach and to keep eating every now and then. (Hadith).

Today there is a hue and cry about the prevalence of diseases but no one, it seems, pays heed to the main cause - overeating. Every one ignores the fact that there are people who eat thrice and four times in a day, some eat four to six times and there are also persons whose mouths remain busy like machines. From the point of view of the Shari'ah such eating comes under the order of abomination or unwarrantableness (na-ja'iz).

Similarly I have come to know some facts about girls in certain countries. For the fear that they would fatten and become plump and flabby by eating well, and then no one would approve and select them for marriage, they avoid eating which they call dieting; but consequently they become weak and unhealthy and suffer from vertigo, anaemia and other ailments. This kind of dieting is also not permissible, because, as said above one should say prayers standing and should have sufficient vitality to observe fasts, and hence to acquire this much strength is incumbent (wajib). So, to feel giddy due to hunger or fall down and sustain injury and to invite a disease by remaining hungry is not permissible.

* * * * * *

XXX

A MUSLIM EATS TO FILL ONE INTESTINE

Hazrat Abd Allah ibn Umar (*razi Allaho anho!*) reports that he heard it from the Holy Prophet (*sallallaho alaihe wa sallam!*) that a Muslim eats to fill one intestine whereas an infidel eats to fill seven intestines. (*Bukhari*, vol. ii, p. 812).

Hazrat Abu Huraira (*razi Allaho anho!*) reports that a man was a glutton but after accepting Islam he used to eat very little. When the Holy Prophet (*sallallaho alaihe wa sallam!*) was told about it, he remarked: "A Muslim eats for one intestine while an infidel eats for seven intestine". (Ibid).

Allamah Qurtubi (Allah's mercy be on him!) has stated that there are seven desires for eating as under:-

(1) Natural desire (2) The desire of the self. (3) The desire of the eye. (4) The desire of the mouth. (5) The desire of the ear. (6) The desire of the nose. (7) The desire of the hunger.

A Muslim eats to satisfy the said hunger but the infidel eats to satisfy all the seven desires. (*Umdat al-Qari*, vol. xxi, p. 42). Hence the mark of a perfect Muslim is that he takes food as per need just to assuage hunger.

The other meaning is that because a Muslim eats after reciting Bismillah, Satan does not share his food and cannot take away the *baraka* of his food and hence his appetite is appeased by eating little; whereas an infidel starts eating without reciting Bismillah and so Satan becomes a sharer and takes away the *baraka* from his food so that he is not easily assuaged and goes on gorging.

The third meaning is that when a perfect Muslim sits down to take his meal, his purpose is to discharge the obligations Allah has imposed upon him and therefore he eats with the concern for the Hereafter. The infidel's purpose, on the contrary, is to nourish avarice, lust, greed, envy, an evil nature and a bad disposition and to live to see the fulfillment of his long hopes. (Ibid). So, a Muslim's intention while sitting down for taking his meal ought to be this that if he acquires strength and vitality by eating, he would use it in discharging Allah's and His slaves' rights; with such intention his eating too would become an act of devotion.

* * * * * * *

XXXI

TO ASCERTAIN BEFORE EATING WHETHER FOOD IS LAWFUL OR OTHERWISE

Imam Bukhari has given the heading (in vol.ii, p. 812) that the Holy Prophet (*sallallaho alaihe wa sallam!*) would not eat as long as the name of the food was not mentioned and would start eating only after knowing it.

Ibn Battal has stated that food was scarce in Arabia and so nothing was considered uneatable, and hence the Holy Prophet (*sallallaho alaihe wa sallam!*) used to inquire the name of the food first. (*Umdat al-Qari,* vol.xxi, p. 38)

Hafiz Ibn Hajar writes that, according to the Shariah, some animals are lawful (for eating) and some are not, and the Arabians of that era did not distinguish the lawful from the unlawful, and hence the Holy Prophet (*sallallaho alaihe wa sallam!*), used to ask the name of the food before eating.

To the Holy Prophet's (*sallallaho alaihe wa sallam!*) dinner-cloth was sometimes brought meat with gravy and sometimes grilled meat and hence he used to enquire about its kind (i.e., about the animal). (*Fath al-Bari,* vol.xi, p. 465).

Warning:- (1) In the present times if one has to visit a town frequently, one should first inquire about the

135

kind of hotel where one wants to dine, because certain hotels use meat of animals (goat, sheep or fowl) which are not slaughtered in the Islamic manner.

(2) Similarly, a pilgrim goes to the holy cities of Mecca and Madina. There, table-fowls, after slaughtering, are dipped in boiling water for plucking. It is impermissible to eat such fowl meat. Hence it is necessary for every one going to another country or city to inquire first about the eatables.

(3) It is impermissible to accept the invitation of those people about whom one knows that their income is illegitimate.

(4) There is scope for accepting the invitation if the earnings consist of both legitimate and illegitimate incomes.

* * * * * * *

XXXII

STATEMENT REGARDING THE EATING OF PUMPKIN

It is recorded in books of Hadith that the Holy Prophet (*sallallaho alaihe wa sallam!*) liked pumpkin. Hazrat Wasilah (*razi Allaho anho!*) reports that Holy Prophet (*sallallaho alaihe wa sallam!*) has advised to eat pumpkin as it increases mental vigour. Hazrat Ayesha (*razi Allaho anha!*) reports that the Holy Prophet (*sallallaho alaihe wa sallam!*) has said: "If there is sorrow in the heart, pumpkin removes it".

It is reported from Hazrat Anas (*razi Allaho anho!*) that pumpkin increases intelligence; he has also reported that the Holy Prophet (*sallallaho alaihe wa sallam!*) amongst all other foods, liked pumpkin. (*Umdat al-Qary*, vol.xxi, p. 62).

* * * * * * *

XXXIII

ON LICKING THE BOWL
AND PLATE

To lick the utensils like the bowl and plate from which
you eat is also an act of sunnah. The Holy Prophet
(*sallallaho alaihe wa sallam!*) has said that the man who
licks his bowl and plate, Allah Most High will fill his belly
in the Hereafter. It is stated in another tradition that if a
man ate from a bowl and then licked it clean, the bowl
would invoke divine pardon for him. It is also reported
that the bowl says: "Even as you protected me from
Satan, may Allah Most Holy protect you also from him"!
The meaning is that Allah bestows upon the bowl the
capacity to speak and then it seeks divine pardon for the
licker. (*Umdat al-Qari*, vol.xxi, p. 77)

A man depending on his reason may think as to how
the bowl or plate both of which have no soul can invoke
divine pardon. The answer to this doubt is that it is not
necessary for the presence or existence of a thing that
man should also see or hear it. Lord Almighty Himself
says in the holy Quran that whatever is there in the
heavens and the earth, it always glorifies Him. Green
trees and green grass laud and praise Allah; white
clothes, as long as they do not become soiled and dirty,
praise Allah. But has man ever listened such lauding and
praising? Hence we should believe the prophetic
statement fully. (*Fayz al-Bari*, vol.i, p. 311).

Does the tongue speak by itself or is it some other
power that makes it speak? If the tongue could speak by

itself, there would have been no dumbness in the world. The Lord Almighty who causes the tongue to speak gives strength to the bowl also and hence it invokes pardon, even as, on the Day of Judgement, hands and feet too will depose regarding man's deeds. (*Vide Sura-e Yasin*).

* * * * * * *

XXXIV

ON HAVING TWO DISHES

Imam Bukhari (Allah's mercy be on him!) has given the following heading: "To Partake Dishes of Two Colours and Two Kinds". And he has recorded a hadith that the Holy Prophet (*sallallaho alaihe wa sallam!*) used to eat cucumber and dates together. (vol. iii, p. 819)

Hazrat Ayesha (*razi Allaho anha!*) says that she used to eat water-melon with dates. It says in another tradition that "my mother used to feed me water-melon with dates so as to make me robust and send me earlier as a bride. I became very healthy very soon due to the said diet". The tradition in the *Nasa'i* says that "I was fed cucumber along with dates therefore I became very healthy". (*Fath al-Bari*, vol.xi, p. 506).

Ima Nauwavi writes that to eat two kinds of fruits and two kinds of dishes (at a time) is permissible and the said traditions also prove that one should take good food.

There is no divergence of opinion among the ulema regarding the said proposition (*mas'ala;* it is quite proper (*ja'iz*) if sometimes two different dishes and some fruits are brought to the dinner-cloth; it is not forbidden. And the abomination that has been reported from the predecessors means that to make it a habit and to gather several dishes and fruits on the dinner-cloth without any religious expediency, just to put on airs and show off one's riches, is abominable. (*Fath al-Bari*, vol xi, pp. 5-6).

Allamah Aiyni, on the authority of Muhallab (*razi Allaho anho!*), writes that Hazrat Umar Farouq (*razi Allaho anho!*) has forbidden from taking more than one kind of dish. It means that one should not be extravagant; if there is another kind of food, it should be given to some needy person or should be used another time. (*Umdat al-Qari*, vol. xi, p. 73)

On the basis of the aforesaid traditions, it is permissible to have pickles, *papah*, *chutney*, *kachumar* (sliced onions with lime juice and coriander or mint leaves, or any other such preparation), and two kinds of dishes; but it is against *adab* (civil mores), for it is one of the signs of pride, extravagance and wastefulness of the opulent whose dining-tables groan with delicacies. Not only one should avoid such things but also refrain from habituating oneself to such delicacies. Today the people grumble about poverty but it is not realised that prodigality and bad habits play a great role in bringing it about. Those who cut their coat according to their cloth never experience trouble and distress.

Hazrat Salmah ibn Habib (*razi Allaho anho!*) reports that one day the Holy Prophet (*sallallaho alaihe wa sallam!*) came to Quba. He was observing fast. Hazrat Aws ibn Khawli (*razi Allaho anho!*) was waiting for the breaking of the fast. When it was time to break the fast, he offered a bowl containing milk and honey to the Holy Prophet (*sallallaho alaihe wa sallam!*). He took it and asked what it was. When he was told that it was milk and honey, he put it down on the floor and said: "I don't say that this thing is prohibited but I also don't drink it due to humility". Then he added: "The man who practises humility for the sake of Allah, Allah elevates him; he who shows pride, Allah breaks his neck; he who squanders money, Allah makes him needy; he who takes the middle path, Allah makes him wealthy and independent of others; and he who remembers Allah much, Allah loves him". (*Umdat al-Qari*, vol. xxi, p. 73).

Read each clause and ponder over it; each one is an invaluable gem. Man should cut his coat according to his cloth and adjusting his expenses according to his income should save himself from loans and interest. Then he will have no need to flatter or be a flunkey of anyone. But due to having forsaken these advices, the whole society is in distress, groaning under mountains of loans and no man or cooperative society is willing to come to its rescue and give it shelter.

May Allah bestow upon us the grace to understand the religion correctly! The prophetic teachings are not confined to prayer and fasting only but they also guide us in every sector of human activity. But, alas! the community, due to its ignorance, is negligent towards these teachings and is thus ruining its religious and worldly life.

Much can be written on this topic but here I cease to add from the *Bukhari* and its addenda. Let us now resume the *Shama'il*.

* * * * * *

XXXV

THE HOLY PROPHET'S
(Sallal'aho alaihe wa sallam!)
CURRY

Hadith 1:- It is reported from Hazrat Ayesha (*razi Allaho anha!*) that once the Holy Prophet (*sallallaho alaihe wa sallam!*) observed: "What a good curry the vinegar is"!

Note:- It is good from this point of view that if requires no labour or trouble and bread can be eaten easily with it; moreover, it is always available, and in worldly subsistence little quantity alone is intended. Besides this, there are many other advantages in vinegar: it is good for poisons, cuts down phlegm and yellow bile, helps digestion and kills stomach worms, and is a good appetizer. However, being cold in property, it proves harmful for certain persons, but from this point of view that this excellent curry can be had at all times, howevermuch it is praised it is conceivable. It is for this reason that it is stated in one hadith that the Holy Prophet (*sallallaho alaihe wa sallam!*) used to take it and used to say: What a good curry it is"! It says in one hadith that he has invoked *baraka* for it and has also stated that it was the curry of the former prophets, too. It is said in another hadith that the house where vinegar is available the occupants thereof are not needy (i.e., they are not in need of any other curry)". (*Ibn Maja*).

Necessary Explanation:- The said hadith does not imply that vinegar is better than all other kinds of curries. Ibn Qayyim (Allah's mercy be on him!) has stated that once when the Holy Prophet (*sallallaho alaihe wa sallam!*) came home, the holy wife offered bread for eating and so he asked if some curry was also there. She replied that there was nothing in the house except vinegar. At this he observed that "vinegar is a fine curry". So it does not imply that vinegar is better than every other kind of curry. Had she offered mutton, milk or honey, he would have praised these things much more. (*Mawahib,* p. 85)

Hadith 2:- Hazrat Nauman ibn Basheer (*razi Allaho anho!*) remarks: "Are you people not, surrounded by delicacies of your hearts" choice, whereas I have seen the Holy Prophet (*sallallaho alaihe wa sallam!*) that the quantity of even ordinary dates used to be not so much that it could sate his hunger".

Note:- The Companion's aim here is to persuade (the people) to conform to the Holy Prophet (*sallallaho alaihe wa sallam!*) and to be content with little of this world. When, in the hadith, a hearty quantity of dates has been negatived, what to say about the availability of bread and curry!

Hadith 3:- Sbu Usayd (*razi Allaho anho!*) reports that the Holy Prophet (*sallallaho alaihe wa sallam!*) said; "Use olive oil for eating and also for massaging because it is the oil of an auspicious tree".

Note:- (1) This auspicious tree grows in Syria - the land of the prophets. (2) Seventy prophets have blessed this tree. (3) Its age is normally one thousand years; it fructifies after it is forty years old. (4) Every part of this tree is useful. (5) The properties and advantages of olive oil have been stated copiously in medical books. It is for these reasons that the use of this oil was recommended.

The auspiciousness of this tree is proven from a Quranic verse : *"Min shajratin mubarakatin zaitunatin"*. Why is it auspicious? As regards this, there are different statements of the ulema. Some say that this tree mainly grows in Syria, the land to which as many as seventy prophets were sent. Some other ulema say that its auspiciousness is due to its many advantages. Abu Nuaym says that there is cure in it for seventy diseases one of which is leprosy. The oil is used for light and as a cooking medium. The ash of its wood is especially useful in washing silk. It is said that the age of this tree is very long; after growing, it bears fruit after forty years and lives upto a thousand years.

Hadith 4:- Hazrat Abu Obayd (*razi Allaho anho!*) reports :--"I cooked mutton for the Holy Prophet (*sallallaho alaihe wa sallam!*). Since he liked the foreleg-meat, I offered him one foreleg. Then he asked for another. I offered it again. Again he asked for another, I said: 'O Apostle of Allah! The goat has only two fore legs'. He said: 'I swear by that Holy Being in whose powerful possession is my life! Had you kept quiet, then, as long as I demanded, forelegs would have continued to come out of this small pot".

Note:- This was a prophetic miracle and a similar incident is quoted from Abu Raf'e in *Musnad-e Imam Ahmed*. It is explicit that this incident happened with both of them. There is no wonder in it for such incidents have happened numerously in the Holy Prophet's (*sallallaho alaihe wa sallam!*) life.

Once Hazrat Abu Ayyub Ansari (*razi Allaho anho!*) invited the Holy Prophet (*sallallaho alaihe wa sallam!*) and Hazrat Abu Bakr Siddiq (*razi Allaho anho!*) for a dinner and prepared only that much food which would have sufficed for only two men. Then the Holy Prophet (*sallallaho alaihe wa sallam!*) asked Abu Ayyub to call thirty noble men from amongst the Ansar. He brought them. Then the Holy Prophet (*sallallaho alaihe wa sallam!*) said: "Now call sixty men". After their having eaten, he again called other men. Thus, totally, one hundred and eighty men partook the food that was meant for only two.

Hazrat Somrah (*razi Allaho anho!*) reports that once mutton was brought in a bowl before the Holy Prophet (*sallallaho alaihe wa sallam!*). Then, from morning till dusk people were coming and eating from it.

Hazrat Abu Huraira (*razi Allaho anho!*) had with him more than ten dates in a bag. The Holy Prophet (*sallallaho alaihe wa sallam!*) asked him if he had any eatable with him. Abu Huraira replied that there were dates in the bag. The Holy Prophet (*sallallaho alaihe wa sallam!*) took out a few dates, recited an invocation on theme and said "Now keep calling ten men at a time and go on feeding them". Thus the dates went round for all the men of the army, and about the remaining dates he said: "Keep eating from it but never turn it (bag) upside down". According to the Holy Prophet's (*sallallaho alaihe wa sallam!*) saying, Abu Huraira kept eating from it during Hazrat Abu Bakr's as well as Hazrat Umar's regimes, even during Hazrat Usman's time; he also used to give away dates from it in charity. But reports Abu Huraira, on the day Hazrat Usman was martyred, a man forcibly snatched the bag from him and the *baraka* too vanished.

Hazrat Anas (*razi Allaho anho!*) reports: "In a Valima-feast given by the Holy Prophet (*sallallaho alaihe wa sallam!*), my mother prepared malidah (pounded bread mixed with ghee and sugar) and offered it in a bowl to him. He asked me to call such and such persons and any one who might meet me in the way. I went out and whoever came across me I kept sending him to the Holy Prophet (*sallallaho alaihe wa sallam!*) until the whole house and the place where the Companions of the Suffa resided were crowded. Then the Holy Prophet (*sallallaho alaihe wa sallam!*) said: "Make batches of ten persons and go on eating". When all the guests had eaten heartily, he ordered the bowl to be picked up". Hazrat Anas exclaims: "I cannot say whether the bowl was fuller before or after all the guests had partaken from it"!

Qazi Iyaz observes that these incidents had taken place in the presence of many people and hence there could be no mistake in the narration of these incidents, for had a narrator committed any mistake, other Companions would have corrected him. The said incidents, therefore, are quite authentic.

Hadith 5:- Hazrat Umm Hani (the Holy Prophet's cousin) reports: "The Holy Prophet (*sallallaho alaihe wa sallam!*) came to me (during the conquest of Mecca) and asked me if there were any eatables in my house. I told him that dry bread and vinegar were there. He said: "Bring them; that house where vinegar may be there is not devoid of curry".

Note:- There is more detail in Hazrat Ibn Abbas's tradition which has been recorded in *Baihaqi,* that the Holy Prophet (*sallallaho alaihe wa sallam!*) asked Umm

147

Hani if there was anything to eat. Umm Hani (*razi Allaho anha!*) said that there was only dry bread and she felt ashamed of offering it to him. He said: 'No! Bring it.' He broke the bread into pieces, dipped them into water and added some salt. Then he asked her if there was any curry. She said there was nothing except vinegar. He sent for it and then, sprinkling it over the crumbs, ate them and thanked Allah.

Allaho Akbar! How simple was the Holy Prophet's (*sallallaho alaihe wa sallam!*) life! Would that Allah Most Glorious, through His grace and the agency of His beloved prophet, had made it our lot too to follow this simplicity! The truth is that, in the Holy Prophet's (*sallallaho alaihe wa sallam!*) eyes, eating and drinking was a matter of constraint to assuage hunger he would eat whatever was ready or available, for to him eating was to sustain life, unlike us to whom life is meant for the necessity of gastronomy while religious engagements have become superfluous. With him the aim of life was to spread religion and make it successful and victorious, and the human needs were satisfied under compulsion.

Necessary Explanation:- The main aim of his holy life was to convey the message of Islam and to teach its beliefs, commandments and devotions to the people, and the essential necessities of life like food, clothes, bed, etc., he kept as per need only, as minimum as possible. In view of their mission of life and its accomplishment, he and his noble Companions had almost renounced repose, comfort and sumptuous food. In the present times, on the contrary, man has made good food, good clothes and a comfortable bed the prime objectives of life and achieve these comforts he is toiling day and night. It is this low aim that is the main cause of the present-day human degeneration. May Allah bestow upon all the right understanding!

* * * * * * *

XXXVI

THE HOLY PROPHET'S
(Sallal'aho alaihe wa sallam!)
ABLUTION AT MEAL TIME

Note:- This is meant the time before or after taking food. The technical ablution (*wuzu*) which is performed at the time of prayer and is a ritual condition for the saying of prayers is known by all. But in the Arabic language the usual washing of hands and face is also called ablution and is known as 'literal ablution.' Two kinds of traditions have been reported in this regard. From some of them it appears that ablution was performed - the literal ablution; and from others it is indicated that it was not performed the ritual technical ablution.

Hadith 1:- It is reported from Hazrat Ibn Abbas (*razi Allaho anho!*) that once when the Holy Prophet (*sallallaho alaihe wa sallam!*) came out from the lavatory, a meal was offered to him and he was asked if he would require water for ablution. He said: "I have been ordered to make ablution only for prayer".

Note:- That is, the indispensability (*wajub*) of the ritual ablution is for prayer only; it is not necessary to make ablution for the purpose of dining or soon after easing oneself. The Holy Prophet (*sallallaho alaihe wa sallam!*) refused for the same reason that it might not be considered necessary to perform ablution after easing nature.

Necessary Explanation:- (1) If one is thinking of saying prayer, then ablution is compulsory, but it is not obligatory to perform it after easing nature, or before taking a meal. (2) To be always clean with ritual ablution is a sign of the perfect believers. (3) The Holy Prophet (*sallallaho alaihe wa sallam!*) performed certain acts to demonstrate and state their permissiveness (*jawaz*) to the ummah. Now it is for the ummah to think which ones of them are permissible and which superior (*afzal*), (4) To be always clean with ablution is praiseworthy (*mustahab*). After easing nature, urination or defecation, one need not perform ablution and one can take one's meal without it; it is permissible. (5) However, the Holy Prophet (*sallallaho alaihe wa sallam!*) will receive more recompense even for his permissible acts because to demonstrate a permissible act by his own practice was necessary for him and hence there is more recompense for his said permissible acts than for thousands of superior works of the ummah. For example, the Holy Prophet (*sallallaho alaihe wa sallam!*) has said that for saying supererogatory prayer sitting the recompense would be half of what one would get for saying it standing. "But you say *nafl* prayer sitting", asked Hazrat Umm Salmah. He said: "You, the individuals of the ummah, will get half recompense whereas I will get the full". It is because it was necessary for the Holy Prophet (*sallallaho alaihe wa sallam!*) to show the method of saying the *nafl* prayer sitting, and hence his saying prayer sitting is much more superior to the thousands and millions of the ummahs prayers, said sitting or standing. Similarly, though water was available, he did not perform ablution in order to teach the ummah that it was not necessary to do so.

Hadith 2:- It is also reported from Hazrat Ibn Abbas (*razi Allaho anho!*) that once when the Holy Prophet (*sallallaho alaihe wa sallam!*) came out after *istanja* (ritual purification), food was brought before him. The Companions asked him if he would not perform ablution. "Have I to say prayer", replied he, "that I should perform ablution"?

Note:- The previous hadith has already stated that it is not necessary to make ablution for dining, but it is, of course, better to be always with ablution, for the effect of external cleanliness reaches the interior also. Hence it is good to make ablution after easing nature as well; it is praiseworthy (*mustahab*).

Hadith 3:- Hazrat Salman Farsi (*razi Allaho anho!*) says: "I had read in the *Torah* that the washing of hands before eating is the cause of *baraka* and I told the Holy Prophet (*sallallaho alaihe wa sallam!*) about it. He also endorsed this practice that the washing of hands before and after taking food is the cause of *baraka*".

Note:- It is possible that there may have been, in the *Torah*, the order of washing hands only once. If it be so, then the order of washing hands twice, before and after meals, will have to be admitted as an order of the Shari'at-e Muhammadiyyah. Or it is also possible, because the Jews have tampered with the commandments of their religion and changes have been made in the text of the Torah, that the order for washing hands again (after meals) may have been expunged.

According to the statement of the ulema, the meaning of *baraka* due to washing hands before taking meals is that the normal quantity of food becomes plenteous in effect, it causes no harm to the diner and the diner is well-satisfied with it. And the meaning of *baraka* due to washing hands after the meals is that the

152

purpose for which the food was taken is fully achieved; it is assimilated by the body, it produces verve and vigour, as also the strength for the cultivation of good morals.

Explanation:- This is also *baraka* that the plenitude caused by the washing of hands for taking the meal with be gladly shared by other persons. If we see that the host has not washed his hands, we might feel aversion in joining him for taking the meal, thinking that his unwashed hands might have affected the food and thus much of the food would be wasted. (2) It is also *baraka* that when hands are washed after finishing the meal, oiliness is removed, which otherwise could attract some poisonous vermin or animal; thus one is served from the hurt of venomous insects.

The Manners for Washing Hands

(1) The hands of a child will be washed first of all because there is greater possibility of filthiness of his hands. (2) Then the hands of the young and then those of the old should be washed for this is the sunnah method (3) After the meal is over, the hands of the old, as a token of respect for them, should be washed first (4) Before starting eating, the host should wash his hands first, and after the meal he should be the last to do so. (5) The hands washed after the meal should be wiped with a handkerchief or towel, but before starting the meal the washed hands, in order to conform to the sunnah method, should not be wiped. To wipe the washed hands before starting eating is undesirable for the reason that if there is dust on the towel or the handkerchief, it may stick to the fingers and then it may reach the stomach with the food.

* * * * * * *

153

XXXVII

THE HOLY PROPHET'S
(*Sallallaho alaihe wa sallam!*)
INVOCATIONS BEFORE AND AFTER MEALS

Hadith 1:- Hazrat Abu Ayyub Ansari (*razi Allaho anho!*) reports:- Once we were present in the Holy Prophet's (*sallallaho alaihe wa sallam!*) service when food was brought. I never saw food like that any time, for when we started eating it looked so plentiful (full of *baraka*) and at the end of eating so devoid of *baraka*. Astonished, I asked the Holy Prophet (*sallallaho alaihe wa sallam!*) about it. He observed: 'We started eating after reciting Bismillah but at the end when such and such a man joined us without having recited Bismillah, Satan also sat down with him for eating'.

Note:- According to the majority of the ulema, Satan too eats like us and there is no improbability about it. In the hadith quoted above the word Bismillah alone is mentioned and hence the reciting of this word alone is sufficient, but it is better to recite the whole Bismillah; and it should be recited somewhat loudly so as to remind a forgetful companion.

Necessary Explanation:- It appears from reading the Holy Prophet's (*sallallaho alaihe wa sallam!*) statements that, like the human beings, Satan too is always on the look out for opportunities to enjoy food and drink, sexual intercourse, and rest. If man omits Bismillah or forgets

154

to recite it, the Enemy take the opportunity by the forelock and become man's partner in his work. Look at the order of the Holy Prophet's (*sallallaho alaihe wa sallam!*) teachings. He has instructed:- First salute and then enter the house; recite Bismillah and then start eating; recite Bismillah before drinking; first make an invocation and then sleep and, similarly, first pray and then have sexual intercourse with the wife. But man came into the house and did not salute. Thus Satan was emboldened to enter the house as well as empowered to indulge in his nefarious activities. Allah's Holy Name was omitted while eating and drinking and so Satan became a partner therein. Invocation was omitted while retiring to bed and thus Satan got a bed also for resting. Similarly, because invocation was not recited before coitus, Satan became a partner in this activity and impaired the seed, and offspring produced by such action, which was shared by Satan came to be called '*mugharreboon*'.

Now just think that Satan got every thing in the house: eatables, water, bed, and every other necessary thing, even one's wife to sleep with. Thus man came fully under Satan's control and became so helpless that he abandoned divine works and began to dance to the Satan's tunes. Hence the best device to take wind out of Satan's sails and enfeeble his immense powers and save oneself from his devilish beguilement is to recite Allah Holy Name, Bismillah, and other suitable invocations and prayers for specific works and occasions.

Hadith 2:- Hazrat Ayesha Siddiqa (*razi Allaho anha!*) reports that the Holy Prophet (*sallallaho alaihe. wa sallam!*) has said that if someone forgets to recite Bismillah and remembers it later let one recite '*Bismillah-e wa Aakherahu*'.

Hadith 3:- Hazrat Umar ibn Abi Salemah (*razi Allaho anho!*) went to the Holy Prophet's (*sallallaho alaihe wa sallam!*) presence. There was food on a dinner-cloth near him. The Holy Prophet (*sallallaho alaihe wa sallam!*) said: "Son I come here and eat with your right hand from before you".

Note:- While the reciting of Bismillah is an act of sunnah according to all the ulema, to eat with the right hand is also an act of sunnah according to a majority of ulema. According to some of them, eating with the right hand is indispensable (wajib), because the Holy Prophet (*sallallaho alaihe wa sallam!*) had cursed a man who was eating with his left hand. This exemplary story is recorded in the books of Hadith. The Holy Prophet (*sallallaho alaihe wa sallam!*) saw a man eating with the left hand and so asked him to eat with right hand, but the obdurate man refused to do so, saying that he could not eat with the right hand. At this the Holy Prophet (*sallallaho alaihe wa sallam!*) said: "May you not be able to eat in future also". I After this incident that man's right hand could not be lifted upto the mouth. Similarly, a woman was seen eating with the left hand. The Holy Prophet (*sallallaho alaihe wa sallam!*) cursed her therefore she died of plague.

Since, according to the majority of the ulema, it is an act of sunnah to eat with the right hand, one should be very careful about it. But now-a-days the people are indifferent to this instruction, particularly for drinking the use of the left hand has become very common - has spread like a contagion. The Holy Prophet's (*sallallaho alaihe wa sallam!*) instruction is: "Eat with the right hand and drink also with the right hand, for Satan eats and drinks with the left hand".

Similarly, to eat from before oneself is an act of sunnah.

Hadith 4:- Hazrat Abu Sa'eed Khudri (*razi Allaho anho!*) reports that the Holy Prophet (*sallallaho alaihe wa sallam!*), after finishing the meal, used to recite the following prayer : "*Al-Hamdo lillahil-Lazi at'amna wa saqana waj'alna minal-Muslimeen*" ("All praise to Allah Who fed us, watered us and made us Muslims").

Note:- Praise to Allah after having eaten, it is obvious, is quite appropriate, for one finished one's meal and assuaged the appetite; moreover, it is also an occasion for thanks giving, for there is a Quranic verse which says: "if you thank Me. I will bestow more on you". And the fact of being a Muslim is joined to it for the reason that the spiritual bounties too may accompany the external bounties; or for this reason that thanksgiving and praising of Allah (on the provision of food and water) are, in fact, the result of Islam itself.

Hadith 5:- Hazrat Abu Omamah (*razi Allaho anho!*) reports that when the dinner-cloth was removed from before the Holy Prophet (*sallallaho alaihe wa sallam!*) he would recite the following invocation :-

"*Al-Hamdo Lillah-e hamdan kathiran tayyiban mubarakan fahe ghaira mawadd'a wa la mustaghna 'anho Rabbana*"

("For Allah Alone are all such praises that have no end, praises free from all evil qualities like hypocrisy, etc. Auspicious is the praise that can neither be omitted nor can be uncared for. O Lord! Accept our thanks").

Hadith 6:- Hazrat Ayesha Siddiqa (*razi Allaho anha!*) reports that once the Holy Prophet (*sallallaho alaihe wa sallam!*) was taking a meal with six men when a bedouin came and finished the whole food in two morsels only. The Holy Prophet (*sallallaho alaihe wa sallam!*) observed: "Had he started eating after reciting Bismillah, this food would have sufficed for all".

Note:- Since the bedouin did not recite Bismillah, Satan also joined with him and finished the food, and caused scarcity.

Hadith 7:- Hazrat Anas (*razi Allaho anho!*) reports from the Holy Prophet (*sallallaho alaihe wa sallam!*) that Allah Most High is very much pleased at this act of the slave that he may thank Allah at every morsel and draught of water.

Summary of the Sunnah Method of Eating

(1) To wash hands before eating is an act of sunnah. (2) One should not wipe one's hands with a handkerchief or towel after washing them for eating (3) The entire Bismillah should be recited before starting eating. (4) Even if the word Bismillah alone is recited the sunnah will be accomplished (5) If one forgets reciting it in the beginning, one may recite "*Bismillah-e Awwalahu wa Aakhirahu*" in the middle or whenever one remembers it. (65) The morsels should be small. (7) One should normally use only three fingers for eating (8) The meal should be taken calmly. (9) One should eat with the right hand. (10) One should eat from before oneself. (11) The morsel should be made from the portion before oneself and from below the food as divine mercy descends upon

158

the surface of the food. (12) If it is a mixed curry of mutton, potato, tomato, pumpkin, etc., it is permissible to pick up pieces thereof from other sides. (13) 'Al-Hamdo lillah' may be recited over each morsel. (14) If a piece or grain falls down it should be picked up and eaten as otherwise Satan would eat it and take away *baraka*. (15) After having taken the meal, one should recite the invocation. (16) By omitting Satan becomes a sharer and the *baraka* is taken away. (17) The vessels (for eating) should be neat and clean. (18) Hands should be washed after the meal and wiped with a handkerchief or towel.

May Allah bestow upon all the grace to act according to the said method! Amen!

* * * * * * *

XXXVIII

THE DESCRIPTION OF THE HOLY PROPHET'S
(sallallaho alaihe wa sallam!)
BOWL

Note:- By bowl is meant, as it appears from the tradition, that bowl with which he used to drink water.

Hadith 1:- It is reported from Hazrat Thabit (razi Allaho anho!) that Hazrat Anas (razi Allaho anho!) took out a wooden bowl, on which was an iron band, and said: "O Thabit! This is the Holy Prophet's (sallallaho alaihe wa sallam!) bowl".

Note:- The ulema have stated this bowl from Hazrat Nazr ibn Anas's legacy had been sold for eight lakh dirhems. Imam Bukhari had drunk water from this bowl in Basra. But some ulema say that this was some other bowl.

Necessary Explanation:- Allamah Baijori has stated (on p. 100 of his book) that besides the said bowl there were other bowls too. Their names are as follows :-

Raiyan, Mughith, Qadh-e Mo'azzab. There was also a glass bowl.

Hadith 2:- Hazrat Anas (razi Allaho anho!) reports that he had served all sorts of potable things, like water,

nabiz, honey and milk, in this bowl to the Holy Prophe
(*sallallaho alaihe wa sallam!*)

Note:- Nabiz is a soft drink made from dates o
raisins. Dates or raisins are immersed in water; when th
water is fully affected by the thing immerse, it is calle
nabiz. It is an exhilarating and invigorating drink. Fo
the Holy Prophet (*sallallaho alaihe wa sallam!*) date
were immersed in water at night and then he used t
drink this water in the morning. Sometimes this wate
was used on the second day, provided there was no fea
of intoxication in it, because anything that produce
intoxication is prohibited (*haram*).

Explanation:- From that very same bowl he woul
drink water, milk, honey, medicine, and also th
invigorating drink nabiz. May Allah bestow upon us to
the grace to adopt such simplicity! Amen!

* * * * * *

161

XXXXIX

THE DESCRIPTION OF THE FRUITS THE HOLY PROPHET
(sallallaho alaihe wa sallam!)
A T E

Hadith 1:- Hazrat Abd Allah ibn Ja'far (*razi Allaho anho!*) reports that the Holy Prophet (*sallallaho alaihe wa sallam!*) used to eat cucumber with dates.

Note:- Cucumber is cold in effect and date is hot. By eating both together, they become temperate. It is also known from this hadith that the nature, property and effect of the eatables should also be considered. Secondly, cucumber is insipid and date is sweet; so when eaten with dates, the cucumber also becomes sweet.

Explanation:- It is certain that the Holy Prophet (*sallallaho alaihe wa sallam!*) did know the properties of things. Since cucumber is cold in property, it can cause cold and catarrh, or to safeguard against any disease that is created by cold the cucumber was taken with date which is hot in its property and any fear of disease that may be caused by heat was expelled by eating dates with cucumber, which then became a temperate food, advantageous to the body.

Similarly, the Holy Prophet's (*sallallaho alaihe wa sallam!*) taking dates with butter is proven, so that the heat produced by dates may be neutralised and may not cause harm to the body. From this auspicious prophetic practice it is proved that by mixing certain things with some eatables, their harm is removed and they become beneficial, and it is also proved that he was a dietician in his own right, knowing the art of selecting wholesome foods and of blending them so as to offset their cold or hot effects and thus make them beneficial to the body and guard it against disease.

Hadith 2:- Hazrat Ayesha (*razi Allaho anha!*) reports that the Holy Prophet (*sallallaho alaihe wa sallam!*) used to eat watermelon with fresh dates.

Note:- There is also this in a tradition in the *Tirmizi* that the Holy Prophet (*sallallaho alaihe wa sallam!*) had observed that "the heat of the dates removes the coldness of watermelon and the coldness of the watermelon offsets the heat of the dates".

Hadith 3:- Hazrat Anas (*razi Allaho anho!*) reports that he had seen the Holy Prophet (*sallallaho alaihe wa sallam!*) eating musk-melon with dates.

Note:- Some ulema have stated that it was watermelon and not muskmelon because the latter is hot in effect. But it is not necessary that one reason may be there at all places. It is possible that because a musk-melon was insipid, he might have eaten it with dates. Today also the insipid fruits are eaten with sugar.

Hadith 4:- Hazrat Abu Huraira (*razi Allaho anho!*) reports that whenever a new fruit arrived, people used to bring it (as a present) for the Holy Prophet (*sallallaho alaihe wa sallam!*), and he used to recite this invocation:-

"Allahumma bark lana fi thamrena wa barik lana fi madinaten wa barik lana fi sa'ena wa bark lana fi

163

modena; Allahumma inna Ibrahima 'abdoka wa nabiyoka wa Khaliloka wa innahu da'aka le Makkata wa inni ad'ooka lil Madinata bemithl-e ma da'aka be-Makkata wa mithlahu ma'hu"

"O Allah! Bestow *baraka* in our fruits, and bestow *baraka* on our cities, and bestow *baraka* on our measures (like) *sa'* and *mod*. O Allah! Verily, Abraham was Your slave and prophet and intimate friend, and verily I too am Your slave and prophet. The invocation (for those things) that Abraham made for Mecca, I also make the same invocation for doubling those things for Madina".

Then he used to call small children and distribute the fruits among them.

Note:- Prophet Abraham's invocation was as under:-

"Faj'al af'edatam minannas-e tahvi ilaihim warzuqhum minath-thamarat."

"Incline the people's hearts towards Mecca and provide them with fruits (for eating)!"

Hadith 5:- Reb'ea (*razi Allaho anha!*) reports :-

"My uncle, Ma'az ibn 'Afra sent me with a tray of fresh dates, on which there were also small downy cucumbers, to the Holy Prophet (*sallallaho alaihe wa sallam!*), who was very fond of cucumbers. When I reached his holy presence with the cucumbers, there were lying near him ornaments that had been brought to him from Bahrain. He picked up a handful of them and gave them to me".

164

Note:- Cucumber besides the aforesaid advantages of its eating with dates, also fattens the body. Accordingly, Hazrat Ayesha (*razi Allaho anha!*) reports that at the time of her departure as a bride from her parents' home to that of her holy and illustrious husband, her mother, wishing he to look a little well grown up, had fed her fresh dates with cucumber and she did gain in plumpness.

The Holy Prophet (*sallallaho alaihe wa sallam!*) is also reported to have eaten cucumber with salt at times, but this is a weak tradition. There is, however, no doubt that sometimes he might have taken it with salt and sometimes with dates, because sometimes one likes to have a sweet thing and sometimes saltish.

* * * * * * *

XL

THE HOLY PROPHET'S
(sallallaho alaihe wa sallam!)
DRINKABLES

It is reported from Hazrat Ayesha (razi Allaho anha!) that amongst drinkables the Holy Prophet (sallallaho alaihe wa sallam!) liked the cold and sweet drink most.

Note:- Apparently by this hadith is meant cold and sweet water and it is also probable that it may be sherbet of honey or nabiz of dates. In the prophetic court no particular attention was paid to eatables - he would eat any edible thing that was available, but special heed was given to cold water. Cold and sweet water was especially brought for him from Sunqya, a place several miles away from Madina. The Holy Prophet (sallallaho alaihe wa sallam!), in the invocation of Prophet David (peace be on him!) reported by him, has also mentioned these words: "O Allah! Bestow upon me such love of Yours that may be greater than my love for life and property, wife and children, and also the love for cold water"!

Hadith 2:- Hazrat Ibn Abbas (razi Allaho anho!) reports as under :-

I and Khalid ibn al-Walid went to the Holy Prophet (sallallaho alaihe wa sallam!) at Hazrat Maimunah's (who was maternal-aunt of both of them) house. She brought milk in a vessel. The Holy Prophet (sallallaho alaihe wa sallam!) drank from it and then told me: "Now the right to drink is yours (because you are on my right side); but if you wish to give it first to Khalid, then give him preference (over yourself)". "I cannot give preference", said I, "to anyone for your leftover". Then the Holy Prophet (*sallallaho alaihe wa sallam!*) said: "Whenever Allah Most High feeds a man any thing, he should recite this invocation: '*Allahumma barik lanna fehe wa at'imna khairum minho*'! ('O Allah! Give abundance (*baraka*) in this and bestow better than this'). And when Allah Most High bestows milk, this invocation should be recited: '*Allahumma barik lana fehe wa zidna minho*'! ('O Allah! Give abundance in it and give more of it'!).

Ibn Abbas (*razi Allaho anho!*) says that the Holy Prophet (*sallallaho alaihe wa sallam!*) taught to invoke for the better of every thing and for more quantity of milk for the reason that, as he said, besides milk there is nothing else that serves the purpose of both milk and water.

Note:- The Holy Prophet (*sallallaho alaihe wa sallam!*) handed the bowl of milk over to Ibn Abbas for the reason that he was on his right side and, according to hadiths, to ply a bowl from the right side is praiseworthy (*mustahab*); and he asked to give preference to Khalid because he was senior in age. The prophetic teaching implied in this was that though one may have the right, one should give preference to the older persons. But for Ibn Abbas the importance of the Holy Prophet's (*sallallaho alaihe wa sallam!*) leftover and his ardour for it prevailed which was due to his extreme love for him. The Holy Prophet's (*sallallaho alaihe wa sallam!*) love was the ruling passion in the Companions' hearts. So Ibn Abbas drank the milk first and then gave it over to Kahlid.

Necessary Explanation:- Ibn Abbas did not give the Holy Prophet's (*sallallaho alaihe wa sallam!*) leftover milk to Khalid for the reason that there must have been some effect of his auspicious saliva in the bowl. The Companions used to scramble for this saliva (*Bukhari*, vol. i, p.26), which smelled like musk (Umdat al-Qari, vol.iii, p. 70)

Allamah Suyuti has related certain traditions regarding the Holy Prophet's (*sallallaho alaihe wa sallam!*) holy and auspicious saliva. Wa'il ibn Hajar (*razi Allaho anho!*) reports that a bucket of water was brought to the Holy Prophet (*sallallaho alaihe wa sallam!*). He rinsed out his mouth in it. Then this bucket of water was poured into a well; or he rinsed out his mouth into the well, therefore the well used to smell of musk.

It is reported from Hazrat Anas (*razi Allaho anho!*) that there was a well in his house into which the Holy Prophet (*sallallaho alaihe wa sallam!*) had spat and thereby its water had become very good. The water of no other well in Madina was as sweet as of this well.

The Holy Prophet's (*sallallaho alaihe wa sallam!*) slave-maid Razinah reports that on the day of Ashura he used to send for sucking or used to send for Hazrat Fatima's (*razi Allaho anha!*) suckling babies and used to put a little of his auspicious saliva into their mouths with the instruction not to suckle them till evening; and this auspicious saliva used to suffice them till then.

Umairah bint Mas'ud (*razi Allaho anha!*) reports :-

We five sisters came to the presence of the Holy Prophet (*sallallaho alaihe wa sallam!*). He was eating a piece of mutton. He took out a piece from his mouth and gave us to eat. Each one of us ate a little of it with the result that our mouths since then have never given bad odour.

Abu Omamah (*razi Allaho anho!*) reports that a woman used to rattle on ceaselessly and unrestrained. She came to the Holy Prophet's (*sallallaho alaihe wa sallam!*) presence. He was eating mutton at that time and so he gave her a piece of it. The woman asked him to give her that piece which was in his auspicious mouth. So he took it out and gave it to her. She ate it up, whereby she became alright, her tongue became controllable and she ceased to run off at the mouth and blather.

Hazrat Aamir ibn Qurayz (*razi Allaho anho!*) reports :-

I brought my son Abd Allah to the Holy Prophet's (*sallallaho alaihe wa sallam!*) presence. The boy was five years old. The Holy Prophet (*sallallaho alaihe wa sallam!*) spat into his mouth. Thereafter (so great a *baraka* was produced in his mouth that) if that boy puffed his breath at a rock, water would issue from it. (*Khasa'is-e Kubra*, p.61-62)

Besides these, there are several other factual stories about the Holy Prophet's (*sallallaho alaihe wa sallam!*) auspicious spittle and tongue. Whenever Hazrat Hasan and Hazrat Husain (when they were small children) cried, The Holy Prophet (*sallallaho alaihe wa sallam!*) used to put his tongue into their mouths; they would suck it and become quiet because they used to receive from it diet like milk and water.

169

Hazrat Abd Allah ibn Abbas (*razi Allaho anho!*) was sitting on his right side and so the leftover milk he gave him first. Thus discharging the due of the rightful person, he also taught to show respect to the elders.

Necessary Explanation 2:-   The Holy Prophet (*sallallaho alaihe wa sallam!*) recommended for Khalid. Recommendation, however, should not constrain man. One should ponder over it and, weighing advantage and disadvantage, adopt what one considers better for oneself. Accordingly, here, too, Ibn Abbas did not feel constrained by recommendation. First he drank the milk himself and then handed it over to Khalid. Hazrat Bariah (*razi Allaho anha!*) was a slave-woman. She was manumitted. After gaining her freedom, she became entitled to annul her *nikah* (marriage-tie). So she broke her *nikah* with her husband, Hazrat Mughith. Due to Mughith's weeping and request, the Holy Prophet (*sallallaho alaihe wa sallam!*) urged Bariah not to dissolve the *nikah* and remain Mughith's wife. She asked him whether it was an order or a recommendation. When told that it was only a recommendation, Hazrat Bariah chose to annul the *nikah*.

This is true democracy and liberty that even a slave-woman and a mere boy should be able to enjoy her/his right. May Allah bestow upon all the grace to understand Islam! Amen!

* * * * * * *

XLII

THE HOLY PROPHET'S
(sallallaho alaihe wa sallam!)
METHOD OF DRINKING

Hadith 1:- Hazrat Ibn Abbas (*razi Allaho anho!*) reports that the Holy Prophet (*sallallaho alaihe wa sallam!*) used to drink the water of Zamzam standing.

Note:- It is forbidden to drink water standing but it is superior to drink the water of Zamzam standing.

Hadith 2:- Hazrat 'Amr ibn Sho'ayb (*razi Allaho anho!*) relates from his father and he from his grandfather that the latter had seen the Holy Prophet (*sallallaho alaihe wa sallam!*) drinking water in sitting as well as standing postures.

Note:- That the Holy Prophet (*sallallaho alaihe wa sallam!*) has forbidden the drinking of water in the standing position is proven from many hadiths. It is stated in the *Muslim* that the Holy Prophet (*sallallaho alaihe wa sallam!*) said that none should drink water standing; should one drink it like that forgetfully, let one vomit it out. This prophetic action (of drinking water in a standing position) and the said prohibition have been reconciled by the ulema in different manners. The opinion of some of the ulema is that the prohibition came later and it therefore abrogates the earlier practice, whereas some ulema assert the very opposite of it: they say that the traditions reporting the drinking of water in a standing position abrogate the prohibition.

171

But the famous assertion is that the prohibition is not a legal and forbidding order but it is by way of civil mores and is also by way of affection and mercy, because Ibn Qayyim and others have shown the harms of drinking water in the standing position. In short, the Holy Prophet's (*sallallaho alaihe wa sallam!*) drinking water standing is just to state the legitimacy of doing so, so that it may be known that to drink water in the standing position is not illegal (*haram*) due to the said prohibition, though it is not good and is abominable.

Hadith 3:- Hazrat Nazal ibn Sabrah (*razi Allaho anho!*) reports that when Hazrat Ali (*razi Allaho anho!*) was sitting in the courtyard of the Mosque of Kufa, water was brought to him in an earthen pot. He, with a handful of water, rinsed out his mouth, sniffed water, and then drew the wet hands on his face, hands and head; then he drank some water in the standing position and exclaimed: "This is the ablution (wuzu) of that man who is already ritually clean with ablution; I saw the Holy Prophet (*sallallaho alaihe wa sallam!*) also doing like this".

Note:- It has been called an ablution in the lexical sense or may be it was interpreted as *masah* (drawing of wet hands over certain parts of the body) because very little water had been used. In some other traditions the washing of hands and feet is also mentioned; if it was so, then it would be called a fresh ablution.

To drink the leftover water of ablution in the standing position is permissible. Allamah Shami, on the authority of certain saints, has reported the drinking of the leftover water of ablution in the standing position to be a tried remedy for the cure of diseases, and Mullah Ali

172

Qari has stated its praiseworthiness (*istahbab*) in his commentary upon the *Shama'il*.

Hadith 4:- Hazrat Anas (*razi Allaho anho!*) reports that the Holy Prophet (*sallallaho alaihe wa sallam!*) used to pause thrice for breathing while taking water and used to call this method to be very pleasant and refreshing.

Note:- To drink water in one breath has been reported to be forbidden. The ulema have stated several harms of drinking water in one breath; they have stated it to be the cause of the weakening of the nerves particularly and it is also the cause of damage to the stomach and the liver.

Hadith 5:- It is reported by Hazrat Ibn Abbas (*razi Allaho anho!*) that the Holy Prophet (*sallallaho alaihe wa sallam!*), while drinking water, used to breathe twice. It is also reported by him that water should be drunk not in one but two or three breaths.

Note:- The meaning of this hadith is that water should be drunk in at least two breaths, or it means that two breaths in drinking and one earlier total up to three.

Hadith 6:- Thamamah (*razi Allaho anho!*) reports that Hazrat Anas (*razi Allaho anho!*) used to drink water in three breaths and used to say that the Holy Prophet (*sallallaho alaihe wa sallam!*) also used to drink like this only.

Necessary Explanation:- The etiquette of drinking: (1) The glass or bowl should be taken in the right hand. (2) Bismillah should be recited before drinking. (3) It should be drunk in three breaths (4) The potable thing

173

should be drunk in a sitting position. (5) At every breath the mouth should be removed form the vessel so as to exhale the breath away from it. (6) 'Al-Hamdo Lillah' should be recited at each pause. (7) If need be, it is permissible to drink in more than three breaths. 98) To imbibe water directly from the tap or the mouth of a leather water-bag is risky as some dangerous or harmful thing might be gulped and it might create diseases; hence a glass or bowl should be used. (9) To drink the water of Zamzam or the leftover water of ablution in the standing position is an act of sunnah. (10) If there is no place for sitting, it is permissible to drink water standing. (11) It is good to drink the leftover water of some other person, for the prophetic statement is that the leftover water of a Muslim is a cure for diseases. (N.B.: One should avoid drinking water immediately after sexual intercourse and any hard work or manual labour). (12) Before drinking the water of Zamzam, one should make an invocation because whatever invocation is made, Allah Most High grants it. (13) If one wishes to give leftover water, milk or sherbet to others, one should begin from the right side, irrespective of the status and position of the person on that side. (14) If tea or sherbet is to be served to guests, it should be begun from the right side of the host. (15) After drinking, thanks should be given to Allah. (16) The leftover water should be drunk.

* * * * * *

XLII

THE HOLY PROPHET'S
(Sallallaho alaihe wa sallam!)
USE OF PERFUME

Note:- Whether or not the Holy Prophet (*sallallaho alaihe wa sallam!*) used a perfume, his auspicious body always emitted a fragrant odour. Accordingly, Hazrat Anas (*razi Allaho anho!*) has reported that never did he smell any fragrance, neither of amber nor of musk nor of any other thing, more delightful and enchanting than that of the Holy Prophet's (*sallallaho alaihe wa sallam!*) body. Many similar traditions corroborate this statement that his holy body always emitted fragrance and people used his perspiration in place of perfume. For instance, Umm Sulaym's tradition is recorded in the *Muslim*, etc., that once when she was the Holy Prophet (*sallallaho alaihe wa sallam!*) asleep and perspiration oozing from his holy body, she began to collect the droplets of perspiration in a phial. He woke up and asked her what she was doing. She said that she would mix it with her perfume as it was more embrosial than any other scent.

Similarly, it has been reported that once the Holy Prophet (*sallallaho alaihe wa sallam!*) whiffed his breath over his hand and drew it over Hazrat Oqabah's waist and stomach wherefore he become so odoriferous that each one of his four wives used to apply a lot of perfume so as to surpass him in fragrance but his aroma always dominated over theirs.

175

Similarly. Hazrat Abu Ya'la and others have reported that if the Holy Prophet (*sallallaho alaihe wa sallam!*) happened to pass through a lane, people coming to it later would find its air so redolent, so full of aura that they would know that he had passed recently through that lane.

Note:- Besides having a natural, inherent pleasant odour the Holy Prophet (*sallallaho alaihe wa sallam!*) always used good perfumes.

Hadith 1:- Hazrat Anas (*razi Allaho anho!*) reports that the Holy Prophet (*sallallaho alaihe wa sallam!*) had a perfume-box from which he used to apply perfume.

Hadith 2:- Hazrat Thamamah ibn Abd Allah (*razi Allaho anho!*) reports that Hazrat Anas (*razi Allaho anho!*) would never turn down perfume, saying that the Holy Prophet (*sallallaho alaihe wa sallam!*), too, never declined a gift of perfume.

Hadith 3:- Hazrat Ibn Umar (*razi Allaho anho!*) reports that the Holy Prophet (*sallallaho alaihe wa sallam!*) used to say that three things must not be declined: (1) pillow, (2) hair-oil-perfume, and (3) Milk.

Note:- The Holy Prophet (*sallallaho alaihe wa sallam!*) prevented from saying no to the acceptance of a gift of these three things for the reason that the gift of any of these three things does not become a burden upon the giver and sometimes declining hurts the giver's good feelings. The implication is that if a man offers a present or gift of small and ordinary things, he should not be said no to; any such gift should be accepted with thanks.

Hadith 4:- It is reported from Hazrat Abu Huraira (*razi Allaho anho!*) that the Holy Prophet (*sallallaho alaihe wa sallam!*) said: "A male fragrance is one the aroma of which spreads but its colour remains invisible (like that of rose *kevda*, etc.) and a female fragrance is that the colour of which may be dominant but its odour is subdued, light (like that of henna, saffron, etc.)

Note:- The meaning is that menfolk should use such hair-oil, attar, scent, etc., which may have fragrance but no tint.

Explanation:- In contrast to the males, the women-folk should used such perfume, hair-oil, powder etc., which may have a tint but may diffuse very light fragrance so that may not reach far to strangers, as otherwise their emotions will be stirred and this might lead one to sin. Colour does not befit the males and therefore they should use only such perfume that may not leave a coloured stain.

* * * * * * *

XLIII

THE HOLY PROPHET'S
(*sallallaho alaihe wa sallam!*)
MANNER OF TALKING

Hadith 1:- Hazrat Ayesha (*razi Allaho anha!*) reports that Holy Prophet (*sallallaho alaihe wa sallam!*) used to be very clear in his talk so that the associates could easily memorise it.

Note:- Whenever he talked, he would not talk volubly so that people would understand it only in parts; he used to talk clearly so that every one present in the majlis could follow him properly.

Hadith 2:- Hazrat Anas (*razi Allaho anho!*) reports that the Holy Prophet (*sallallaho alaihe wa sallam!*) sometimes used to repeat (as per need) his talk thrice so that his hearers might follow him thoroughly.

Note:- Whenever the Holy Prophet (*sallallaho alaihe wa sallam!*) used to state a difficult problem or talked about an important matter, he used to repeat it thrice, or, if the audience was large and the voice could not reach all, he repeated it thrice. To repeat thrice was the limit, otherwise sometimes, as per need, he simply repeated the talk once only.

Hadith 3:- Hazrat Imam Hasan (*razi Allaho anho!*) reports :-

I requested my maternal-uncle, Hind ibn Abi Halah, who very often used to describe the Holy Prophet's (*sallallaho alaihe wa sallam!*) characteristics, to narrate before me his mode and nature of talking. He said: "The Holy Prophet (*sallallaho alaihe wa sallam!*) was always concerned (as regards the Hereafter), always meditating (regarding Allah's Essence and Attributes) or reflecting about the ummah's welfare, and due to these matters he never enjoyed relief and freedom from anxiety. Very often he used to be quiet and would not talk unless very necessary. His whole talk used to be well articulated, condensed and in concise words and each talk used to be distinct from the other (absolutely free from absurdities and ambiguities). Neither he was irascible nor would ever humiliate any one. However much little may be a divine bounty, he would consider it great and would never speak ill of it. Of eatables he would never speak ill nor would praise them too much. As regards the world and worldly matters he never took offence but if someone exceeded the limit in respect of religious matter or a truth, then no one could withstand his wrath nor prevent it until he avenged it, though for his own person he would be neither angry with any one nor try to be avenged of it. If, due to some reason, he had to point out towards any direction, he used to do so with his whole hand. Whenever he felt astonished at some thing, he used to turn his hand, and while talking, he would also gesticulate and sometimes would strike the right palm against the inner part of the left finger. When he felt angry with anyone, he used to turn his face from him and either paid no attention towards him or excused him; and when he felt happy, he would as if close his eyes with modesty. Most often his laughing was no more than smiling, and when he laughed his auspicious teeth appeared like bright white hail-stones".

Necessary Explanation:- (1) Unlike men of straw, the Holy Prophet (*sallallaho alaihe wa sallam!*) was never free from anxiety; he used to remain immersed in the contemplation of Allah and His attributes and in the care of the Hereafter. He was always absorbed in the thought of that responsibility in the world Allah had entrusted to him. (2) It was the Holy Prophet's (*sallallaho alaihe wa sallam!*) miracle that his talk used to be succinct (fewer words that carried more meaning) and, at that, he would not talk unless it was absolutely necessary. (3) He always talked clearly - without omitting words here and there so as not to make his stalk incomprehensible to others. He never put on airs but always talked informally, in a simple, clear manner. (4) He never showed impoliteness and discourtesy to any one; even while giving advice, he used to preserve decorum. While advising in a majlis, he scrupulously refrained from mentioning anybody's name so as to avoid disrespect to anyone. but used general terms, usually in the plural sense (for instance: what is the condition of the community that it should commit such acts'?) No individual was mentioned by name. (5) About worldly matters and as regards his own person he never became angry nor gave any punishment. (6) He punished only those people who spoke or did anything against the religion, but only after their fault was proved by witnesses. As regards punishment, he did not accept anybody's recommendation. (7) Those worldlings who are eaten with pride often point towards something with their fingers but the Holy Prophet (*sallallaho alaihe wa sallam!*) would use his whole hand to do so. For Divine Unity alone he used to make a sign with his finger and for all other works he used the whole hand. (8) His auspicious teeth emitted light.

In view of the fact that mental powers of all are not equal and all the audience cannot be on the same intellectual plane, he often used to repeat his words thrice in order to instil the purport of his talk into the minds of his Companions; and he used to speak the same thing twice and thrice if the audience was large, turning his face to the right and the left also.

* * * * * *

XLIV

THE HOLY PROPHET'S
(*sallallaho alaihe wa sallam!*)
LAUGHTER

Hadith 1:- Hazrat Jabir (*razi Allaho anho!*) reports that the Holy Prophet's (*sallallaho alaihe wa sallam!*) auspicious calves were thin and his laughter was no more than a smile. "Whenever I met him", says Jabir, "I used to think that he had applied collyrium to his eyes but in fact he had not applied it".

Note:- The edges of the eyelids had a natural tint of collyrium and hence it looked as if he had applied collyrium.

Hadith 2:- Abd Allah ibn Harlth (*razi Allaho anho!*) reports that he did not see any one more smiling than the Holy Prophet (*sallallaho alaihe wa sallam!*).

Note:- It means that he was habituated to smiling rather than laughing.

Hadith 3:- Jarir bin Abd Allah (*razi Allaho anho!*) reports that "the Holy Prophet (*sallallaho alaihe wa sallam!*) never prevented me, from attending his majlis after my embracing Islam, and whenever he saw me, he used to laugh (or, as stated in another tradition, smile)"

Hadith 4:- Aamir bin Sa'd reports that his father Sa'd told him that the Holy Prophet (*sallallaho alaihe wa sallam!*) laughed on the day of the Battle of the Ditch so that his auspicious teeth became visible. Aamir says that he asked why`he had laughed. Sa'd said that a pagan was carrying a shield and though Sa'd was a greater archer, the pagan, moving the shield this side and that, was protecting his forehead (i.e,, he was dodging Sa'd's arrow though Sa'd was a reputed marksman of his time). Once Sa'd took out an arrow, nocked it in the bow and, having strung it, was waiting to shoot. As soon as the pagan raised his head from behind the shield, Sa'd shot so accurately that the arrow did not miss the mark. Instantaneously the pagan fell down and his legs lifted up. The Holy Prophet (*sallallaho alaihe wa sallam!*) laughed. at this incident. Aamir asked his father what particular thing was in it at which he laughed. Sa'd said "At my action".

Note:- Since there had been suspicion that he might have laughed at the sudden baring of the victim's *satr* because of the lifting of the legs; hence Aamir had to ask this question again. But Sa'd clarified that the Holy Prophet (*sallallaho alaihe wa sallam!*) did not laugh at this; he laughed at Sa'd's marksmanship despite the pagan's dexterity in shielding himself to save his life.

Necessary Explanation:- Though always immersed in thought, the Holy Prophet (*sallallaho alaihe wa sallam!*) often smiled to please his doting and devoted Companions. The slight movement of the lips in smile indicated to the Companions that they were welcome. If he had kept himself engrossed in his anxiety and contemplation, the Companions would have thought that he was not pleased by their coming and was rather inconvenienced by it. So, setting aside his anxieties and contemplative mood, he used to welcome them with a pleasant smile; moreover, to console or show kindness to a visitor is also a form of devotion. Smiling is just a relaxing of features by parting lips slightly into a pleased expression. (2) Laughing is the making of sounds and movements of face and sides by which a lively amusement or sense of exultation, etc. is instinctively expressed. In laughing the teeth also become visible due to the parting of the lips. One hears the sound oneself; others cannot. The Holy Prophet's (*sallallaho alaihe wa sallam!*) laughing over certain affairs of the Hereafter is proven. (3) But laughing aloud and long is not fully proven in his case. (4) A prayer is not vitiated by smiling. But it becomes invalid by laughing and hence one must perform fresh ablution and say it again. (5) A prophetic statement to the effect that too much laughing destroys the lustre of the face and deprives the heart of its vitality.

May Allah bestow upon us grace to follow the prophetic instructions!

* * * * * *

XLV

THE HOLY PROPHET'S
(*sallallaho alaihe wa sallam!*)
WIT AND HUMOUR

Note:- The Holy Prophet's (*sallallaho alaihe wa sallam!*) play of wit (*mizah*) is proven, and, at the same time, as has been recorded in the *Tirmizi* from Ibn Abbas's narrative, he has also prevented from cracking jokes. Imam Nauwavi has reconciled this hadith in this way that to habituate oneself to excessive joking which may harden the heart or may prevent from the remembrance and thought of Allah or may hurt the feelings of a Muslim or involve disrespect to him is on no account permissible in Islam; only that pleasantry which is free from the above-mentioned defects and is meant merely for mutual cheering up and delight is praiseworthy (*mustahab*) and permissible, as has been reported by Abd Allah ibn Harith (*razi Allaho anho!*) that he did not see a more mirthful person than the Holy Prophet (*sallallaho alaihe wa sallam!*).

Moreover, mirthfulness was especially necessary for the Holy Prophet (*sallallaho alaihe wa sallam!*) because his personal dignity was so great and of such magnitude that his awesomeness reached a distance of a month's journey. Therefore, if he had not cared to smile and indulge in pleasantries it would have become difficult for the people to associate with him, all the ways of benefitting from him would have been closed, and, moreover, all the great Shaikhs (spiritual preceptors) and august men, who would continue to come till the

185

Day of Doom and who painstakingly try to conform to him, would have deliberately avoided smiling and mirthfulness, and this mode of theirs would have created several difficulties for their attendants. May Allah Most High send unlimited blessings and mercy to that holy being who bequeathed the routes of convenience for his ummah!

Someone remarked to Sufyan ibn Aiyniyah, a great traditionist (*muhaddith*) that "joking too is a calamity". He reported that "it is rather a sunnah, but for one who knows its occasions and can cut good jokes".

Hadith 1:- Hazrat Anas (*razi Allaho anho!*) reports that once the Holy Prophet (*sallallaho alaihe wa sallam!*) called him: "O the owner of two ears"!

Note:- All have two ears. There must have been some special reason for calling him like that. May be he had large ears or had a keen faculty of hearing so that he could hear a distant voice.

Hadith 2:- Hazrat Anas (*razi Allaho anho!*) reports:

Whenever the Holy Prophet (*sallallaho alaihe wa sallam!*) met us, he used to pass witty remarks. Accordingly, I had a younger brother. To him he used to say: "*Ya Aba 'Umayr! Ma fa'iun-nughayr*"? "O Aba Umayr! Where's gone your nughayr"?).

Note:- Nughayr is the name of a bird. The ulema have translated it as 'lal' (name of a very small bird). Al-Damiri, the author of *Hayat al-Haiwan*, has translated it as 'bulbul'.

186

Imam Tirmizi says that the Holy Prophet (*sallallaho alaihe wa sallam!*) called the child by a cognomen (*kunyah*) the necessity for which arose from the fact that boy had reared a bird which had died and so the boy was sitting in a sorrowful condition. Hence, just to cheer up the boy, the Holy Prophet (*sallallaho alaihe wa sallam!*) jocularly asked him as to what had happened to his pet Nughayr.

Some ulema have derived more than hundred propositions (*masa'il*) from this hadith and have shown more than hundred advantages from it. May I be sacrificed over that holy being from whose single jocular remark more than hundred propositions have been derived!

Hadith 3:- Hazrat Abu Huraira (*razi Allaho anho!*) reports that the Companions asked: "O Apostle of Allah! You also crack jokes with us"! "Yes, but I do not speak lies:, he replied.

Hadith 4:- Hazrat Anas (*razi Allaho anho!*) reports that a jungle-resident named Zahir ibn Haram always used to bring, whenever he came, presents of the jungle, like vegetable, etc., for the Holy Prophet (*sallallaho alaihe wa sallam!*), and when he thought of returning from Madina, the Holy Prophet (*sallallaho alaihe wa sallam!*) used to give him presents of urban eatables. Once the Holy Prophet (*sallallaho alaihe wa sallam!*) remarked: 'Zahir is my jungle and I am his city." Zahir was somewhat ugly but the Holy Prophet (*sallallaho alaihe wa sallam!*) had a particular attachment to him. Once Zahir, standing somewhere, was selling his goods. The Holy Prophet (*sallallaho alaihe wa sallam!*) came silently behind him and grasped him in such a way that he (Zahir) might not see him. Zahir said: "Who's there?

Leave me." But when he saw through the corners of his eyes that it was the Holy Prophet (*sallallaho alaihe wa sallam!*) himself, he very carefully pressed his back against his chest and began to rub it. The Holy Prophet (*sallallaho alaihe wa sallam!*) then said: "Who's there who may buy this slave?" "O Apostle of Allah"! said Zahir, "if you sell me off, you will find me defective and will fetch little price." "No", said the Holy Prophet (*sallallaho alaihe wa sallam!*), "in the sight of Allah you are not defective; on the contrary, you are very precious".

Hadith 5:- It is reported from Hazrat Hasan Basri (Allah's mercy be on him!) that an old woman came to the Holy Prophet's (*sallallaho alaihe wa sallam!*) presence and said: "O Apostle of Allah! Please pray Allah may enter me into Paradise". "Old women", said he, "cannot enter Paradise". The old woman started to go away weeping. Then he said: "Tell that woman that she will not enter Paradise in her aged condition but Allah will make all the women of Paradise young virgins".

Necessary Explanation:- Indulging in humour and pleasantries is permissible provided it is according to facts; but if somebody's heart is pained or feelings are hurt or there is possible of quarrel, then it is not humour; it is jeering and jesting, for it is meant to humiliate the other person and hence it is prohibited (*haram*). Allah Most High says in the Holy Quran: "O ye who believe! Let not a folk deride a folk who may be better than they (are), nor let women (deride) women who may be better than they are". (XLIX: 11). It is for this reason that deriding, buffoonery, jeering etc, are prohibited (*haram*). Only such jocularity, jocosity, banter, ready wit, repartee, witticism, wordplay and smart sayings are permissible that are meant to please or cheer up someone. In the above-mentioned hadith a fact was stated that old men and old women will not be sent to Paradise in their dotage and senility but will be sent there as young men and young women.

* * * * * * *

XLVI

THE HOLY PROPHET'S
(*sallallaho alaihe wa sallam!*)
REMARKS REGARDING
POETIC VERSES

Note:- A verse is a speech which is deliberately made metrical and rhyming. It is proven from the holy Quran that the Holy Prophet (*sallallaho alaihe wa sallam!*) was not at all a poet, because when the pagan Arabs called him a magician, a poet, a madcap, a maniac, etc. the Quran described these false imputations with much amazement and emphatically denied and refuted these by saying :-

"And We have not taught him (Muhammad) poetry nor it is meet for him". (XXXVI: 68).

So, whenever verse-like phrases are quoted in the Holy Prophet's (*sallallaho alaihe wa sallam!*) speech, we will prove that these occasional metrical and rhyming-words escaped his lips unintentionally, off hand, and hence they cannot be called verses or couplets proper because couplets are composed intentionally.

"According to this humble writer (Maulana Zakariya Sahib), this too is a miracle that in spite of the fact that the Holy Prophet (*sallallaho alaihe wa sallam!*) was not a poet, sometimes he did extemporise verses and hence one has to admit that had he really been a poet, he would have certainly composed the most genuine and exquisite poetry, for he was not helpless in this matter, but Allah

190

Most High had made him too great a person to be a poet. Many traditions have been reported in praise and dispraise of poetry. It appears from some of them that poetry is a good thing and from others that it is not. The truth, however, is that poetry in itself is neither good nor evil; if the theme is good, it is good, and if the theme is not good, it is evil and, therefore, forbidden.

N.B.:- But it has been reported from a large number of ulema that even though the themes and contents of poetry be good, it is certainly not good to be engrossed in it all the time.

Hadith 1:- Someone asked Hazrat Ayesha (*razi Allaho anha!*) if the Holy Prophet (*sallallaho alaihe wa sallam!*) sometimes recited couplets "Yes, sometimes", replied she, "for instance, he used to recite a verse of Abd Allah ibn Rawaha (*razi Allaho anho!*) and a times couplets of other poets' also by way of example; e.g., the following verse of Tarfa:-

"*Wa yateeka bil-akhbar-e mal-lam tuzawwad*" meaning "sometimes even that man whom you did not pay any remuneration for it brings news to you". That is, sometimes, in order to know the news of a place, one has to pay salary or bear expenses of journey to send a man to that place for ascertaining facts, but sometimes it so happens that a man comes and delivers all kinds of news to one at one's home without having to be paid for this service.

Note:- Some ulema have asserted that in this hadith the Holy Prophet (*sallallaho alaihe wa sallam!*) has described his own example that "I narrate to you at your homes and without having charged any fees, the particulars about Paradise, Hell, the Hereafter, the Day of Judgement, the past prophets and the future events and yet these infidels do not derive any benefit from these things".

In this hadith have been mentioned two poets: (1) Hazrat Abd Allah ibn Rawaha who was a well-known Companion; he had become a Muslim even before the Holy Prophet's (*sallallaho alaihe wa sallam!*) emigration (*hijrat*) and had been martyred in the Battle of Muta before the Holy Prophet's (*sallallaho alaihe wa sallam!*) eyes. (2) Tarfa is a famous Arab poet of the pre-Islamic era. In the famed literary work entitled *Sab'a Mu'alliqa* (The Seven Suspended Poems), the second *qasida* is from his pen. Tarfa could not survive upto the advent of Islam.

N.B.:- A wise poetical aphorism of a non-Muslim is permissible for quotation.

Hadith 2:- It is reported from Hazrat Abu Huraira (*razi Allaho anho!*) that the Holy Prophet (*sallallaho alaihe wa sallam!*) remarked: "The trust maxim that a poet may have uttered is this saying of Labeed ibn Rabee'ah: "*Ala kullo shai'in ma khala Allaho batilan*" meaning: "Beware! Besides Allah, everything of this world is perishable".

Note:- Labeed (*razi Allaho anho!*) was an illustrious poet. After embracing Islam, he had renounced composing poetry. He used to say: "Allah hath given me a better change for poetry". He lived for more than one hundred and forty years.

Hadith 3:- It is reported by Hazrat Jundub ibn Abd Allah (*razi Allaho anho!*) that once the Holy Prophet's (*sallallaho alaihe wa sallam!*) finger was injured by a

192

stone and became blood-stained. At that time he has recited a verse, which means: "You are only a finger that has got covered with blood; but this flow of blood will not go waste because this injury has been sustained in the way of Allah - it will merit recompense".

Note:- The majority of ulema have stated that this Incident took place in the Battle of Ohad; according to some, it had occurred earlier - before the Hijrat.

Hadith 4:- Hazrat Ayesha (razi Allaho anha!) reports that the Holy Prophet (sallallaho alaihe wa sallam!) used to get a pulpit placed in the mosque for Hazrat Hassan bin Thabit (razi Allaho anho!) so that, standing on it, he used to recite verses in the Holy Prophet's (sallallaho alaihe wa sallam!) praise or give a smashing reply in verse to the infidels who used to slander the Holy Prophet (sallallaho alaihe wa sallam!). And the Holy Prophet (sallallaho alaihe wa sallam!) also used to say: "Allah Most High also helps Hassan through the Holy Ghost as long as he helps the religion".

Note:- Jihad has been waged in every period in a different and distinct manner. During the prophetic times it was waged with the sword as the last resort because the obdurate and implacable enemies of Islam, instead of listening to reason, were bent upon exterminating Islam. Jihad is a wide term; the other kind of jihad was verbal in which couplets and panegyrics were recited to gain victory over the opponents.

Necessary Explanation:- The votaries of Islam should ponder over the above note. Jihad is not only waged with the sword but it is waged in other ways also. The effort and endeavour that is made for the elevation of Allah's Name and keeping it aloft is also jihad. Hence

193

the same effort and toil that is required on the field of battle is also required in writing books and delivering lectures to refute the charges that the detractors of Islam are wont to level against it. The intellectual among the people are habituated to reading books, journals and treatises; they are aggrieved when they come across silly charges and strange objectives imputed to it by the enemies of Islam; they, therefore, wish to be enlightened as regards the true teachings of Islam, and hence it is also a jihad of sorts to render every kind of correct guidance to such seekers of truth. Hazrat Hassan used to reply to the infidels in verses which he recited from the pulpit in the Prophet's Mosque. The Holy Prophet (*sallallaho alaihe wa sallam!*) has remarked that these verses inflicted deeper wounds on the pagans than the arrows could inflict. Hence, it should be known that all kinds of worriors are required to defend and serve Islam; they, too, who are busy in replying to the Jews' and Christians' false accusations, are serving and fighting for Islam.

* * * * * * * *

XLVII

THE HOLY PROPHET'S
(*sallallaho alaihe wa sallam!*)
STORY-TELLING AT NIGHT

Hadith 1:- Hazrat Ayesha (*razi Allaho anha!*) reports that, one night, when the Holy Prophet (*sallallaho alaihe wa sallam!*) related a story to the holy wives, they exclaimed that it was like that of Khorafa. He, therefore, enquired from them if they knew what Khorafa's real story was. Khorafa was a man who belonged to the Banuu Ozrah, a tribe of Yemen. Once he had been kidnapped by the genii, who had kept him with them for a number of years. When they brought him back among the human beings, Khorafa used to narrate the genii's strange actions, habits, customs, manners of eating and drinking, etc., before the people. The people used to wonder at these narrations and hence they began to call every wonderful and amazing story Khorafa's story.

Note:- Probably his name was Khorafa or because his stories were considered myths, he was nicknamed Khorafa.

The genii were very powerful prior to the advent of Islam; they used to trouble human beings very much. They used to kidnap women also for sexual purposes; many such stories are well-known. Several stories of the genii's weeping at the Holy Prophet's (*sallallaho alaihe wa sallam!*) birth are extant in books. Allamah Suyuti has recorded a number of such stories in his book, *Khasa'is-e Kubra.* The genii were so powerful that they could reach the skies to eavesdrop the talks there. But after the Holy Prophet's (*sallallaho alaihe wa sallam!*) advent, their power and sway had much diminished.

Explanation:- Imam Bukhari has recorded the hadith, named *Hadith-e Umm* Zor'a, in which eleven women narrate particulars about their respective husbands' under the heading Husn-e Mua'shirat ("Living Nicely With One's Wives"). Imam Tirmizi, too, has used the same heading here.

As the said heading itself indicates, the import of this hadith is that (1) one should live nicely with one's wife or wives. To please them, one should sometimes tell them stories also, even as the Holy Prophet (*sallallaho alaihe wa sallam!*) sometimes amused his holy wives with stories. (2) And imitating the Holy Prophet (*sallallaho alaihe wa sallam!*), one should behave politely with one's wives (Mawahib, p. 136) (3) The Holy Prophet (*sallallaho alaihe wa sallam!*) has forbidden talking after the Isha prayer, but, as it appears from the said heading given by Imam Tirmizi under which he reports that the Holy Prophet (*sallallaho alaihe wa sallam!*) narrated two stories, it is permissible to talk with one's wives after the Isha prayer, for the show kindness to every one is also a form of devotion; and as such, to have regard for the wives' sentiments and to try to please them is also a devotion. (4) Similarly, to talk with a guest after the Isha, just to show kindness to him, is also permissible after Isha. (6) To kill time in idle talk and gossiping and to sit in friends' company just for joking and buffoonery is not permissible; it is from such things and talks that Holy Prophet (*sallallaho alaihe wa sallam!*) has forbidden. Now-a-days the way the young people waste their time is prohibited (*haram*). (7) To describe the wrongdoing of a man or woman, without naming either, for the sake of advising, is permissible.

Hadith 2:- In the *Hadith-e Zor'a*, eleven women, making a pledge, sat down to narrate truthfully, the good and bad points of their respective husbands.

But no one knew these women nor their husbands. Hence it is known from this that to describe the bad characteristics of a person whom no one knows is permissible; it is not forbidden and it does not come under back-biting.

* * * * * * *

XLVIII

THE HOLY PROPHET'S
(Sallallaho alaihe wa sallam!)
SLEEP

Hadith 1:- Hazrat Br'a ibn 'Aazib *(razi Allaho anho!)* reports that the Holy Prophet *(sallallaho alaihe wa sallam!)*, after lying down for sleeping, used to put his right hand under right cheek and used to recite the following invocation :

"*Rabb-e qini 'azabaka yauma tab'atho 'abadak*"!

("Lord! Save me from torture on the Day of Resurrection"!)

Note:- It appears from this hadith that it was the Holy Prophet's *(sallallaho alaihe wa sallam!)* usual habit to sleep on his right side, and it is hence that it is praiseworthy *(mustahab)* to sleep on one's right side. The other point of wisdom in it is that since the human heart is located on the left side, it remains in an upper position if one sleeps on one's right side; thus one does not sleep very soundly and remains alert even during sleep. If one sleeps on the left side, the hearts remain downward and one sleeps like a log; some physicians, therefore, call it better to sleep on the left side because a sound sleep helps the digestion. This is correct. But they have not considered one harm involved in it: it is this that when the heart remains downward, the weight of the whole body will be upon it and this might engender some disease (of the heart). Hence, to sleep on the right side is more beneficial. Besides this, there are many other points of wisdom in it. For instance, by sleeping on the right side one is reminded of sleeping in the grave after death, and the remembrance of death which too has been insisted upon, has had in it several worldly and religious advantages. It is therefore much better to lie on the right side.

Hadith 2:- Hazrat Huzaifa (*razi Allaho anho!*) reports that the Holy Prophet (*sallallaho alaihe wa sallam!*) after lying down on his bed, used to recite the following invocation:-

"*Allahumma be-ismeka amuto wa ahya*" ("O Allah! I die (i.e., sleep) with Your name and will be alive (i.e., rise up) with Your Name");

The import of this prayer at the time of retiring to bed is that one should remember one's death, for death is just like sleep, and take an account of one's good and bad deeds performed during the day.

Hadith 3:- It is reported from Hazrat Ayesha (*razi Allaho anha!*) that when the Holy Prophet (*sallallaho alaihe wa sallam!*) lied down on the bed, he would join both the hands as they are joined for invocation and breathing over them and reciting *Sura-e Ikhlas* and the *Ma'oozatayn* would the hands all over his body - as far as they could reach. This he used to do thrice, beginning from the head, then face and the front part of the body and then the rest of the body.

Note:- The Holy Prophet's (*sallallaho alaihe wa sallam!*), reciting different invocations at bed time is proven. It is also proven that he used to recite different suras of the holy Quran; it is reported in one hadith that the man who recites any sura of the Quran at bedtime, an angel is appointed by Allah to guard him till his rising up.

Similarly, the Holy Prophet's (*sallallaho alaihe wa sallam!*) reciting the *Alif-Lam-Mim Sajdah* and *Tabarakal-lazi* is also proven; as also the *Ayat al-Kursi* and the last two verses of the *Sura-e Baqra*. And it is reported by one Companion that he was advised to recite *Qul Ya Ayyahul Kaferoon* always at bedtime. Besides these, there are many other invocations which the Holy Prophet (*sallallaho alaihe wa sallam!*) used to recite before sleeping'.

Hadith 4:- It is reported from Hazrat Abu Qatadah (*razi Allaho anho!*) that whenever the Holy Prophet (*sallallaho alaihe wa sallam!*) had to make a halt in a journey in the last hours of the night he used to sleep on his right side, but if he had to halt before dawn, then he would raise his right hand put his head on it and took rest.

Note:- It is clear from this hadith that he would take a nap only when there was more time but contented himself with rest only if the time was short.

Necessary Explanation:- When, after the day's work, man retires to bed for sleeping, the prophetic instruction and teaching is that he should first remember Allah, because sleep is like death and the Holy Prophet's (*sallallaho alaihe wa sallam!*) reciting an invocation that reminds one of death is proven: "O Allah! I sleep with Your Name, through Your power; if I am overtaken by death in my sleep, have mercy upon me". Such invocations in which thanks have been given to Allah are also proven. A sleeping man and a dead man both are alike. Hence the Holy Prophet (*sallallaho alaihe wa sallam!*) has advised to recite *Ayat al-Kursi* before sleeping, as this will protect the reciter from thieves and other mischievous and hurtful things. Enemies usually take advantage of man's inattention and somnolence, and hence the Holy Prophet (*sallallaho alaihe wa sallam!*) has advised to recite the last two suras of the Quran: *Sura-e Falaq and Sura-e Nas*. After reciting these two suras the drawing of the hands over the body is proven. During his fatal illness he did not have the strength to recite these two suras; so Hazrat Ayesha (*razi Allaho anha!*) recited these and drew her auspicious hands over his holy body. The said act implies that one should rather rely upon Allah's omnipotence than upon one's own scheme, understanding and strength, and should entrust his life and wealth to Him for He Alone is the Best Protector. A Muslim's attention should always turn towards Him: while lying down for rest or sleep as well as while rising up from bed.

(2) Since sleep produces unconsciousness both in the eyes and the heart and the limbs of the body become loose, the ablution is invalidated by sleeping, according to the Hanafite rite (*mazhab*).

(3) The Holy Prophet (*sallallaho alaihe wa sallam!*) has said: "My eyes sleep but the heart does not; it remains awake". (Hadith). It was because the chain of revelation (*wahy*) from Allah to the Holy Prophet (*sallallaho alaihe wa sallam!*) continued. Had his heart too slept he could not have remembered the. It was in fact his miracle that his heart always kept awake - even during sleep. Hence the ulema have stated that the Holy Prophet's (*sallallaho alaihe wa sallam!*) dream was a proof (*hujjat*) and not an argument (*dalii*) whereby propositions (*masa'il*) are proved; whereas the dream of

a member of the ummah is not a proof (*hujjat*) and hence propositions cannot be proved from it. (4) Since his heart remained awake, sleep did not invalidate his ablution; had there been any reason that invalidates the ablution, he would have come to know of it. Hence it is mentioned in the next chapter that describes his Tahajjud prayer that he used to stand for this prayer as soon as he got up from sleep because he had already performed ablution before retiring to bed.

* * * * * * *

XLIX

THE HOLY PROPHET'S
(Sallallaho alaihe wa sallam!)
DEVOTIONS

Every movement and rest of the Holy Prophet
(sallallaho alaihe wa sallam!) was a devotion. He was
immaculate and every human error that he might have
committed had been pardoned and he had been given
the good tidings of Paradise in this very world, and yet
he was very careful about saying supererogatory *(nafl)*
prayers. But we, alas!, commit hundreds of sins day and
night as well as cause others to commit them and yet we
neither fear Allah nor engage ourselves in devotions to
Him! Through Allah's grace and bounty, even if we
perform some devotions, our intentions lack sincerity
(ikhlas) and thus render these devotions too useless and
unfruitful, for it is stated in a hadith that recompense
for every work depends upon intention and sincerity. It
is for this reason that the Holy Prophet *(sallallaho
alaihe wa sallam!)* has said that when a man completes
his prayer, only one-tenth of its recompense is recorded
for him, and for still others it is only one-eight, one-
seventh, one-sixth, one-fifth, one-fourth, one-third, and
one-half. *(Abu Da'ud)*. It is reported in one tradition that
the very first enquiry on the Day of Judgement will be
about prayer. Allah will ask the angels to look into His
slaves' prayers whether they are complete or otherwise.
If one's prayer-account is complete, it will be so recorded
in one's register, and if it is incomplete, the angels will
be asked to see if there are any supererogatory prayers
on record. If *nafl* prayers are there, the deficiency in the

Similarly other devotions like zakat, fasting, etc. will also be reckoned. (*Abu Da'ud*).

Now it is for us to see and assess how sincerely we say the obligatory prayers.

Hadith 1:- It is reported from Hazrat Mughira ibn Sho'abah (*razi Allaho anho!*) that the Holy Prophet (*sallallaho alaihe wa sallam!*) used to say such long prayers that his auspicious legs used to swell. The Companions, therefore, would ask him: "Since Allah Most High hath pardoned all your sins, why do you toil so much"? "When Allah hath bestowed on me," he would reply, "so many favours, should I not thank Him (profusely)"?

Note:- This is a lesson in thanksgiving from the Holy Prophet (*sallallaho alaihe wa sallam!*) to the ummah. If one wishes to win more and more pleasure of Allah, it is obvious that one should engage oneself in devotions more and more.

Hadith 2:- It is reported from Hazrat Aswad ibn Yazid (*razi Allaho anho!*) as follows:-

I inquired from Hazrat Ayesha (*razi Allaho anha!*) about the Holy Prophet's (*sallallaho alaihe wa sallam!*) night-prayers as to what was his practice regarding these. She said: "After the Isha prayer he used to take rest in the early part of the night. Thereafter he would say the *Tahajjud* prayer until the last part of the night when he would also say the *Vitr*. Then he used to retire to bed, and, if he desired, he would have intercourse with any one of the wives. Then, after the Fajr prayer-call (*azan*), he would take bath, if necessary, otherwise would only perform ablution and go for the Fajr prayer.

Hadith 3:- It is reported from Hazrat Ibn Abbas (*razi Allaho anho!*) that the Holy Prophet (*sallallaho alaihe wa sallam!*) used to say thirteen *rak'ahs* of *Tahajjud* and *Vitr* together.

Note:- That is, ten *rak'ahs* of *Tahajjud* and three of *Vitr*. Some ulema have stated that these ten *rak'ahs* of *Tahajjud* included two sunnah *rak'ahs* of the Fajr prayer. That is, according to this opinion, he used to say eight *rak'ahs* in the *Tahajjud* prayer.

Hadith 4:- Hazrat Ayesha (*razi Allaho anha!*) reports that sometimes he would not say the *Tahajjud* prayer due to some disability. The *Chasht* (forenoon' prayer) he used to say in twelve *rak'ahs*.

Note:- Since the *Tahajjud* prayer was obligatory for him, it is known from this hadith that he had to miss it sometimes. And if the *Tahajjud* prayer was not obligatory for him, then it is proved from this hadith that the making good of this prayer in the day (at *Chasht*) was meant by him to show its merit to the people. It is also proved from this hadith that if one cannot accomplish one's usual devotional practice at night due to some disability, one can accomplish it during day.

Hadith 5:- It is reported from Abu Salaimah that he asked Hazrat Ayesha (*razi Allaho anha!*) as to how many *rak'ahs* of *Tahajjud* the Holy Prophet (*sallallaho alaihe wa sallam!*) used to say in the holy month of Ramazan. "In the holy month of Ramazan", she replied, "as well as in the other months, he did not say more than eleven *rak'ahs* of *Tahajjud*" (i.e., eight *rak'ahs* of *Tahajjud* and three of *Vitr*).

205

Note:- It is proved from this hadith that the Holy Prophet (*sallallaho alaihe wa sallam!*) always used to say eleven *rak'ahs* in the *Tahajjud* prayer. From some traditions, however, it appears that he used to say thirteen *rak'ahs* also. The answer the ulema have given to this question is that mostly he said eleven *rak'ahs* in *Tahajjud* but sometimes thirteen also.

Hadith 6:- It is reported from Hazrat Huzifa (*razi Allaho anho!*) that once when he said a night-prayer in the Holy Prophet's (*sallallaho alaihe wa sallam!*), company his holliness recited the following invocation:-

"Allaho Akbaro Zul-Malakuto wal-Jabaruto wal-Kibriya-e wal-Azmat". Then (after reciting the *Sura-e Fatiha*) he recited the *Sura-e Baqrah* and performed the genuflexion (ruku'), which was as long as the 'standing' (*qiyam*), and in the genuflexion he went on reciting *"Subhana Rabbe'yal Azim".* Then he stood up and this standing (*qiyam*) was as long as the genuflexion. Then he glided into prostration (sajdah) in which he went on reciting *"Subhana Rabbe'yal 'Aala",* and this prostration too was as long as the standing. Then, rising up from prostration, he sat and went on reciting *"Rabbighfirli".* In short, the Holy Prophet (*sallallaho alaihe wa sallam!*), in this prayer, recited *Sura-e Baqarah, Sura-e Aal-e Imran, Sura-e Nisa, Sura-e Ma'ida* or *Sura-e An'aam.*

Note:- It appears from this hadith that the Holy Prophet (*sallallaho alaihe wa sallam!*) had recited four suras in four *rak'ahs,* a fact which is corroborated by the tradition of the Abu *Da'ud* also; but from the tradition in the *Muslim* and other books (of hadith) it seems that he had recited *Sura-e Baqrah, Sura-e Aal-e Imran* and *Sura-e Nisa,* all the three suras in one *rak'ah* only. So it

206

is quite possible that one time he may have recited all the four suras severally and sometime together.

Hadith 7:- It is reported from Hazrat Ayesha (*razi Allaho anha!*) that once, in the *Tahajjud* prayer, the Holy Prophet (*sallallaho alaihe wa sallam!*) was reciting a single verse repeatedly.

Note:- The verse that he recited like this is from the last section (*ruku'*) of the *Sura-e Ma'ida*.

Hadith 8:- Hazrat Ayesha (*razi Allaho anha!*) reports that the Holy Prophet (*sallallaho alaihe wa sallam!*), during weakness, used to recite more sections of the Quran in the supererogatory prayers (nawafil), and hence he used to say these prayers sitting, and before performing the genuflexion when thirty to forty verses were left he used to recite them standing, thereafter he performed the genuflexion and then glided into prostration; and the second rak'ah too he performed likewise.

Note:- The majority of the ulema proved from this hadith that it is permissible for that man who says the prayer sitting to stand up for genuflexion and prostration. Similarly, according to the majority opinion, it is permissible that a man saying the prayer standing may sit down to perform genuflexion and prostration; and, according to some ulema, it is permissible for only that man who says the prayer sitting to rise up for performing the genuflexion and prostration.

N.B.:- But it should be remembered that this method is permissible only for the *nafl* prayer and not for the obligatory prayers in which sitting is not permissible for one who can say the prayer standing, because standing (*qiyam*) is obligatory.

Note:- *Khasa'il-e Nabavi:* p. 160:-

There is consensus among the Ahl-e Sunnah wal-Jama'ah that the *Taravih* prayer is a sunnah; no one denies this save the Rawafiz. It is clearly and unambiguously stated in the books of Fiqh of all the four imam, namely, Imam Abu Hanifa, Imam Shafi'i, Imam Malik, and Imam Ahmed ibn Hanbal, that *Taravih* of 20 *rak'ahs* is an "insisted sunnah" (*sunnat-e mu'akkidah*)

Imam Malik's famous rite (*mazhab*) in this regard consists of 36 *rak'ahs*. As for Imam Ahmed's, it is stated in his famous book, *Mughni*, that 20 *rak'ahs* are the sunnah. The same is the rite of Sufyan Thauri, Imam Shafi'i and Imam Abu Hanifa.

Since Imam Malik's rite insisted upon 36 *rak'ahs*, the king's envoy came to him with the request to curtail the *rak'ahs* of the Taravih, but the Imam refused to do so and insisted on 36 *rak'ahs*. My teachers used to say that the people in the holy Madina used to say 20-*rak'ah* *Taravih*. But it is praiseworthy to pause in each *taraviha* (intermission for a brief rest) so much that one may say four *nafl rak'ahs* and hence these people used to say four *nafl rak'ahs* in each *taravih* and thus these sixteen *rak'ahs* during the intervenient taravihs totalled to 36 *rak'ahs* of Taravih. However, Imam Malik alone asserts 36 *rak'ahs*, whereas the other three Imams insist on 20 *rak'ahs* only.

* * * * * * *

L

THE DESCRIPTION OF
THE CHASHT PRAYER

Note:- According to the jurisprudents (fuqaha) and the traditionists (*muhaddathin*) any prayer said after the Fajr prayer and the passage of the abominable time, till the sun reaches the meridian, is reckoned as the *Chasht* prayer. But according to the Sufia, the name of the prayer said 20 minutes after sunrise is *Ishraq* Prayer and subsequently any prayer till the sun reaches the meridian is *Chasht* Prayer. The time for the former last upto one-fourth part of the day and the next one-fourth part till noon is the time for the latter.

Many hadiths have been reported for the *Chasht* prayer; they have been narrated by nineteen prominent Companions, though in the *Awjaz* as many as twenty-five Companions have been quoted.

It says in one hadith that there are 360 joints in the human body and it is, therefore, necessary to give alms for each joint every day, and, it says further, "the two *rak'ahs* of *Chasht* prayer will be alms for all the 360 joints."

Hadith 1:- Hazrat Mo'azah inquired from Hazrat Ayesha (*razi Allaho anha!*) if the Holy Prophet (*sallallaho alaihe wa sallam!*) used to say the *Chasht* prayer. "Yes", she said. "He used to say (at least) four *rak'ahs* of *Chasht* and more than these too he said when he liked".

209

Note:- The *Chasht* prayer is a *nafl* prayer. Hence, at the least one should say two *rak'ahs* and for saying more than that there is no limit. Of one's own volition if one says more *rak'ahs*, one is entitled to do so, but the Holy Prophet (*sallallaho alaihe wa sallam!*) used to say twelve *rak'ahs*, which is proven.

Hadith 2:- Hazrat Abu Sa'eed Khudri (*razi Allaho anho!*) reports that 'sometimes the Holy Prophet (*sallallaho alaihe wa sallam!*), used to say the *Chasht* prayer so assiduously that we used to think that now he would never give up saying this prayer, and sometimes he would discontinue it so that we would think that now he would never say it again".

Note:- The Holy Prophet (*sallallaho alaihe wa sallam!*) used to discontinue certain works, as in the case of the *Chasht* prayer, for the convenience of the Ummat-e Muhammadiyyah.

Hadith 3:- Hazrat Abu Ayyub Ansari (*razi Allaho anho!*) reports that the Holy Prophet (*sallallaho alaihe wa sallam!*) used to say four *rak'ahs* of prayer at noon constantly. So he asked him: "You are very particular about saying these four *rak'ahs*"? He replied: "Yes. The doors of the sky remain open, beginning from the decline of the sun upto the Zuhr time and so I wish that some good act of mine may reach the skies, and hence I always say this prayer". Abu Ayyub asked: "Is the qir'at (reading) done in all the four *rak'ahs*"? "Yes, the Quran is recited", said he. When asked if 'salam' ('peace') is said at the end of each two *rak'ahs*, he said: "No, all the four *rak'ahs* are said with one 'salam'.

Note:- This prayer is called *Salat al-Zawal* by the Sufis. According to them, this prayer is counted among the praiseworthy prayers.

According to the majority of the traditionists these are the sunnah *rak'ahs* of Zuhr because, after the decline of the sun, there are no *nafl* prayers, except the sunnah *rak'ahs* of Zuhr which the Holy Prophet (*sallallaho alaihe wa sallam!*) used to say regularly.

Necessary Explanation:- What may I write about the Holy Prophet's (*sallallaho alaihe wa sallam!*) prayer and devotions? Let alone the prayer and devotions – which were true to the core and real - he had turned even his eating, drinking and sleeping into devotions.

It was so because it is his own statement that "works depend upon intention". So if the intention in eating, drinking and sleeping is to give rest to the tired body and remove weakness so that one may engage oneself in prayer with fresh vigour and peacefully, this also amounts to, rather is, devotion. Besides the statement regarding the correctness of intention, he also said: "The coolness of my eyes consists in prayer". So, if the wind started blowing fiercely or the clouds thundered menacingly, his mind was drawn towards prayer; if there occurred a solar or lunar eclipse, he hastened towards the mosque for prayer.

Saying the *Ishraq, Chasht, Awwabin* and *Tahajjud* prayers, he taught the ummah that by saying these prayers besides the obligatory ones, they too can register their names in the list of the recipients of special divine favours. May Allah bestow upon all Muslims, men and women, the grace to aspire for entry in this list through action and practice! Amen!

* * * * * * * *

211

LI

THE DESCRIPTION OF
THE HOLY PROPHET'S
(*Sallallaho alaihe wa sallam!*)
SAYING NAFL PRAYERS
AT HOME

Note:- To say *nafl* prayers at home is praiseworthy because it is proven from the Holy Prophet's (*sallallaho alaihe wa sallam!*) practice; and there are many expediencies in doing so. (1) There will be prosperity (*baraka*) in the home due to the blessedness of prayer (2) The inmates of the house too may learn and cultivate the zest for saying prayers. The Holy Prophet (*sallallaho alaihe wa sallam!*) has remarked: "Make not your homes graveyards". That is, even as prayer is not said in the graveyard or even as the dead cannot say prayers, you also should not make your homes graveyards by not saying (*nafl*) prayers there.

Hadith 1:- It is reported from Hazrat Abd Allah ibn Sa'd (*razi Allaho anho!*) that when he inquired from the Holy Prophet (*sallallaho alaihe wa sallam!*) whether it was better to say the *nafl* prayer at the mosque or at home, he replied: "You know how near is my house to the mosque so that it causes me no inconvenience to come to it, even then I like it more to say the (*nafl*) prayer at home than at the mosque".

Note:- Since the *nawafil* are based on concealment, it is superior to say them at home so that the

212

concealment of which is not proper should be said in the mosque only; for instance, the 2-*rak'ah* prayer at the time of circumambulating the ka'ba.. Although the Taravih prayer is not among the obligatory prayers, it is a special distinctive feature of the auspicious Ramazan and to say it in a congregation is an act of sunnah; similarly every other prayer which is said congregationally e.g., the prayer for eclipse, because the purpose is to reveal these prayers and hence it is better to say them in the mosque.

Necessary Explanation:- To say the sunnah and *nafl* prayers at home is better but due to ignorance such prayers (namazis) are likely to be taunted; or, if one goes home, one will be involved in the home-affairs and will not get time to say the *nafl* prayers there; hence it is better to say the sunnah and *nafl* prayers also in the mosque.

* * * * * * * *

LII

THE DESCRIPTION OF
THE HOLY PROPHET'S
(Sallallaho alaihe wa sallam!)
FASTING

Note:- The Holy Prophet (*sallallaho alaihe wa sallam!*) was habituated to fasting much; sometimes he would go on fasting for several days, because there are many expediencies in fasting. For example, (1) fasting creates sympathy for the hungry; (2) it breaks the animal and libidinous vigour, and (3) creates spiritual power. It is for such reasons that fasting has been made obligatory in almost every religion and all great prophets used to fast. Prophet Noah fasted every day throughout the year, Prophet David fasted every alternate day and Prophet Jesus fasted every third day (i.e., the day of fasting was followed by two successive days of non-fasting).

Hadith 1:- It is reported from Abd Allah ibn Shaqiq (*razi Allaho anho!*) that when he asked Hazrat Ayesha (*razi Allaho anha!*) about the Holy Prophet's (*sallallaho alaihe wa sallam!*) fasting, she replied; "At times the Noble Prophet (*sallallaho alaihe wa sallam!*) went on fasting so much that we thought that on no day in that particular month he world omit it, and sometimes he used to cease fasting completely. But after migrating to Madina he did not fast throughout a month excepting the month of Ramazan".

214

Hadith 2:- Hazrat Umm Salmah (*razi Allaho anha!*) reports that, save Sha'ban and Ramazan, she did not see the Holy Prophet (*sallallaho alaihe wa sallam!*) fasting throughout two consecutive months.

Hadith 3:- Hazrat Ayesha (*razi Allaho anha!*) reports that besides the month of Ramazan, she did not see the Holy Prophet (*sallallaho alaihe wa sallam!*) fasting in any other month so much as in the month of Sha'ban.

Note:- The Holy Prophet (*sallallaho alaihe wa sallam!*) used to fast more in the month of Sha'ban for the reason that it is an auspicious month in which all the deeds of man are submitted before Allah Most High.

Hadith 4:- It is reported from Hazrat Abd Allah ibn Mas'ud (*razi Allaho anho!*) that the Holy Prophet (*sallallaho alaihe wa sallam!*) used to fast on the first three days of every month, particularly on Fridays.

Note:- (1) Insistence has been made in several hadiths on fasting for three days in each month, because each virtuous act merits tenfold recompense. Thus the recompense of three fasts equals to that of a whole month's and, with this reckoning, one can achieve the recompense of fasting throughout one's life time.

(2) As regard the three days on which the Holy Prophet (*sallallaho alaihe wa sallam!*) used to fast, there are different interpretations of the ulema. At times he used to fast on the first three days of a month, at others he fasted on each Monday and Thursday of the month, and sometimes on the 13th, 14th and 15 of the month.

215

Hadith 5:- Abu Sauleh (*razi Allaho anho!*) reports that he inquired from Hazrat Ayesha (*razi Allaho anha!*) and Hazrat Ummm Sulaym (*razi Allaho anha!*) as to which work the Holy Prophet (*sallallaho alaihe wa sallam!*) liked most. Both of them replied: "That work which one may do perseveringly, though it may be very small, very ordinary".

Necessary Explanation: The heading Imam Bukhari has given to this topic (vol. i, p. 11) is: "Of All Works The Most Approved By Allah Is One Which Is Done Persistently". It means man should spare some time daily for devotions: one may recite the *Darud* daily at least a hundred times or recite the *Tasbihat-e Fatima* daily after each one of the five time prayers or read eight to ten sections (*ruku'*) of the holy Quran daily. Such small but persistent acts count much in Allah's sight. Some people, in a sudden burst of religious fervour, devote themselves very enthusiastically to devotional exercises for a fortnight, a month or a couple of months and go abroad for a 40-day term of preaching and self-education, but when the fervour cools down, they give up everything. Such works, done by fits and starts, irresolutely, are not liked by Allah.

Imam Ghazali has observed that if a drop of water falls constantly on a slab of stone, it will make a hole in it in five or ten years; but if twenty or twenty-five thousand buckets of water are poured on the same slab at a time, no hole will be made. Hence a little act of devotion which man can do persistently and maintain till death is more approved by Allah.

Persistence in devotions will achieve for man very high ranks in the Hereafter through the Beloved Lord's approval. So, a little devotion, a small act of virtue, however, small and whatever it is, ought to be done perseveringly and should not be given up, thinking it to be small and insignificant.

It is for this reason that there is a dictum well-known among the Sufi circles that "steadfastness is superior to a thousand miracles"; i.e., to lead life according to the sunnah is better than the performing of a thousand miracles. The recognizability and distinction of man consists inn his conformance to the sunnah, not in possessing miraculous powers.

* * * * * * * *

LIII

THE DESCRIPTION OF THE HOLY PROPHET'S
(Sallallaho alaihe wa sallam!)
RECITATION (TILAWAT) OF THE HOLY QURAN

Hadith 1:- Abu Ya'la (*razi Allaho anho!*) is reported to have said that he inquired from Hazrat Umm Salmah (*razi Allaho anha!*) about the Holy Prophet's (*sallallaho alaihe wa sallam!*) reciting of the Quran. She said: "He used to articulate each word of the recitation (qir'at) distinctly".

Hadith 2:- It is reported by Hazrat Umm Salmah (*razi Allaho anha!*) that the Holy Prophet (*sallallaho alaihe wa sallam!*) used to recite each verse separately. He used to pause after reciting "*Al-Hamdo Lillah-e Rabbil-aalimin*". Then he would pause after reciting "*Ar-Rahmanir Rahim*", then after reciting "*Malik-e Yaumiddin*".

Hadith 3:- Abd Allah ibn Qays (*razi Allaho anho!*) reports that he asked Hazrat Ayesha (*razi Allaho anha!*) whether the Holy Prophet (*sallallaho alaihe wa sallam!*) used to recite the Quran in a subdued voice or loud tone. She replied that he used to recite both ways.

Note:- That is, the Holy Prophet (*sallallaho alaihe wa sallam!*) has used both the methods for the convenience of the ummah; or it is possible that to create avidity in the *ummah* for reciting the Quran he used to recite loudly in the congregation and in a subdued voice when he was alone; or when it did not inconvenience the people, he recited loudly and when it might cause inconvenience, he recited it gently.

Hadith 4:- It is reported from Qatadah (*razi Allaho anho!*) that Allah Most High had endowed every prophet with a handsome face and a beautiful voice. Similarly, the Holy Prophet (*sallallaho alaihe wa sallam!*), too, had a handsome face and a beautiful voice; and he did not recite the Quran like a song.

Necessary Explanation:- The veneration of the holy Quran is binding upon all. Hence, both men and women, when they read it, should read each verse clearly, articulate each word of the verse, and should try and take pains in vocalising the *madd* (the mark put over the letter *alif* to prolong its sound), *ghunna* (sound of the nasal *nun*), *makhraj* (the guttural sound), etc; but one should avoid singing tones. Each syllable, each word and each verse should be articulated with simplicity. (1) In the holy month of Ramazan the hafizes, in their speed of recitation, skip over letters in the Taravih. This is not permissible. It is then better to say the *Taravih* from "*Alam-tara*". (2) One may read or recite loudly or in gentle tone as the occasion may demand. If it is apprehended that it will cause disturbance to sleeping persons or distraction to those busy in praying, remembrance (*zikr*) or spiritual contemplation (*miraqiba*), then one should read or recite sotto voce. Similarly, one should recite it gently if there is fear of showing off or gaining fame. If the said harms or taints are not there and the purpose is to induce and stimulate others, that seeing one they too would read the Quran, then it is superior to read or recite the Quran loudly.

219

The Holy Prophet (*sallallaho alaihe wa sallam!*) has said that its example is like that of giving charity which gains in superiority according to the occasion.

* * * * * * *

LIV

THE DESCRIPTION OF THE HOLY PROPHET'S
(Sallallaho alaihe wa sallam!)
WEEPING

Note:- Man usually weeps due to certain reasons:-

(1) Sometimes he weeps due to the feeling of mercy and kindness. (2) sometimes due to fear (3) sometimes due to love, (4) sometimes due to utmost joy, (5) sometimes due to some pain, (6) sometimes due to grief and sorrow, (7) sometimes due to suffering tyranny and oppression, (8) sometimes the committing of a sin moves him to tears (9) One sort of weeping is due to hypocrisy - to please the present persons. (10) Another kind of weeping is that for which one is hired to wail and lament with praises of a dead person; etc., etc. The Masha'ikh have stated that one kind of weeping is patently false: to cry over a sin and yet persist in it.

The Holy Prophet's (sallallaho alaihe wa sallam!) weeping was mainly due to feelings of mercy and kindness for a dead person or due to anxiety for the ummah or due to Allah's fear of His love, as can be known from the traditions and these kinds of weeping alone are laudable.

Hadith 1:- It is reported from Abd Allah ibn Shikhir (razi Allaho anho!) that once when he went to the Holy Prophet (sallallaho alaihe wa sallam!), he found him

221

saying prayer and due to weeping such a sound was coming from his chest as comes from a boiling casserole.

Hadith 2:- Hazrat Abd Allah ibn Mas'ud (*razi Allaho anho!*) reports as follows:-

Once the Holy Prophet (*sallallaho alaihe wa sallam!*) asked me to recite the Quran to him. I said: "O Apostle of Allah! The Holy Quran has been revealed to you and you ask me to recite it to you"! "It is my wish", he said, "that I hear it from some other person". So I began to recite, beginning from the *Sura-e Nisa*, and when I reached this verse: "But how (will it be with them) when We bring of every people a witness, and We bring the (O Muhammad) a witness against these" (IU:41), I chanced to glance at his auspicious face and saw that tears were rolling down from his eyes.

Note:- This weeping was due to the magnificence of the Holy Quran, for Imam Nauwavi has observed that to weep while reading or reciting the Quran is the habit of the men of Allah. The other reason for weeping here is the description of the Day of Judgement which called before his mind's eye the picture and condition of the Great Assize and caused him to weep. Or it was due to his constant anxiety regarding the ummah that he was moved to tears on hearing this verse.

Hadith 3:- It is reported from Hazrat Ibn Abbas (*razi Allaho anho!*) that one of the daughters of the Holy Prophet (*sallallaho alaihe wa sallam!*) was on the verge of death. He took her in his lap and placed her before himself and in this condition she breathed her last before his eyes. Umm Aiman (*razi Allaho anha!*), his slave-woman, began to cry loudly. So he said to her: "Why did you start wailing before the Apostle of Allah"? Since his own tears too were flowing, she said: "Aren't you also weeping"? "This kind of weeping", said he, "has not been forbidden by the Shari'ah, because the flowing of the tears from the eyes is a mercy of Allah".

Note:- That is, as this hadith shows, the Holy Prophet (*sallallaho alaihe wa sallam!*) had a soft heart. The hardness of heart is the very opposite of the virtue of kindness.

Hadith 4:- It is reported from Hazrat Anas (*razi Allaho anho!*) that the Holy Prophet (*sallallaho alaihe wa sallam!*) was present at the grave of his daughter, Umm Kulthum, and tears were flowing from his eyes. Then he said: "Let only that man who may not have had sexual intercourse with his own wife tonight descend into the grave". At this Hazrat Talha (*razi Allaho anho!*) said that he was such a man, and then he descended into the grave.

Note:- Here has come the Arabic word "*lam yoqarif*", which has been interpreted differently: (1) may not have had sexual intercourse, (2) may not have committed a sin, and (3) may not have talked after the Isha prayer.

Explanation:- (1) It is proved from this hadith that only virtuous, religious men should be allowed to descend into the grave. (2) It is permissible to visit a grave, for it reminds the visitor of the ultimate end. (3) To weep over the death of a daughter or son gently, without wailing and tearing clothes, though tears may flow from the eyes, is permissible. (4) It is permissible to weep on remembering death in the graveyard (5) Talking about worldly matters in the graveyard hardens the heart.

* * * * * * **

LV

THE DESCRIPTION OF THE HOLY PROPHET'S
(*Sallallaho alaihe wa sallam!*)
B E D

Hadith 1:- Hazrat Ayesha (*razi Allaho anha!*) reports that the Holy Prophet's (*sallallaho alaihe wa sallam!*) bedding was made of leather, stuffed with the bark of date-palm.

Note:- The Holy Prophet's (*sallallaho alaihe wa sallam!*) bedding was made of leather and from some hadiths it appears that it was made of sackcloth and sometimes it was a mere mat of palm leaves.

It is proven from many hadiths that whenever the Companions requested him to get prepared a bed of soft material, he used to tell them: "What need is there for me to acquire the satisfaction of this world? My example is like that traveller who, walking on the road, takes rest under a tree". Similarly it is reported from Hazrat Ayesha (*razi Allaho anha!*) that once an Ansari woman came to her and saw that a cloak (generally black in colour and made of goat's hair) was spread as a bed for the Holy Prophet (*sallallaho alaihe wa sallam!*). "Then she went back, prepared a bed wadded with wool and seat it to me for the Holy Prophet (*sallallaho alaihe wa sallam!*). When he came home and saw it lying there, he asked what it was. I told him that an Ansari woman had come and she, on seeing his bed, had sent this one. He asked me to return it. As it looked good to me, I did not want to return it, but he insisted and said: "By Allah! If I wish, Allah Most Glorious will send me mountains of gold and silver. So I returned it".

Hazrat Abd Allah ibn Mas'ud (razi Allaho anho!) reports: Once I went to the Holy Prophet (sallallaho alaihe wa sallam!). He was resting on a sackcloth, which had welted his body. Seeing this I began to weep. He said: "Why are you weeping"? said : "The Caesars and Chosroes, the kings of Byzantium and Iran, sleep on carpets of silk and velvet and you have to take rest on sackcloth! I weep because of this." He said: "There is no need of weeping over it" (for the world is for them and for us is the Hereafter).

Hadith 2:- Imam Muhammad Baqir (Allah's mercy be on him!) reports that someone asked Hazrat Ayesha (razi Allaho anha!) as to what kind of bed there was at her place for the Holy Prophet (sallallaho alaihe wa sallam!). She said: "There was a sackcloth which I used to fold double and spread it for him. One day I thought that if I gave it four folds, it would become softer; so I made it like that. The next morning he asked me what I had spread for him last night. I replied that it was the same old daily bed but last night I had folded it four times. He said: "Let it be as usual, for last night its softness prevented me from saying the Tahajjud prayer".

Note:- That is, he could not wake up for the Tahujjud prayer or he was delayed in saying it at his usual time. It is obvious that one gets sound sleep on a soft bed, whereas it is not so sound and long on a sack cloth.

Explanation: The Holy Prophet (sallallaho alaihe wa sallam!) had been sent to this world as a pattern, a paragon, an exampler, and hence he used to remain away from riches, worldly goods, comfort, luxuries, soft clothes and cosy bedding.

He used to adopt different ways to explain the disadvantages of these things to the ummah. Here, by his own example in the above-mentioned hadith, he wants to drive home the fact that one does not like to get our of a cosy, comfortable bed – even for an obligatory prayer. The implication is self-evident: that well-padded, soft beds should be, as far as possible, avoided. (2) The Holy Prophet's (*sallallaho alaihe wa sallam!*) straitened circumstances were self-imposed; poverty he had chosen for himself voluntarily and, therefore, he wanted that all his personal belongings (clothes, bedding, food, etc.) should be commensurate with his self-adopted poverty. Even if he received soft beds as presents, either he would return them to the givers or to some poor, needy persons. The example of silken clothes is there; he used to give away such clothes to his Companions. (3) He did not approve of having more than the necessary number of beds. It is stated in one hadith that one bed is for man, the second is for the wife, the third for the guest and the fourth is for Satan. That is, he has stated the evil of possessing surplus beds; if there is a redundant bed, Satan will take rest on it or it is a hint towards increase in the possessor's pride, pomposity and ostentation. (*Mawahib*, p. 161).

* * * * * * *

LVI

THE HOLY PROPHET'S
(Sallallaho alaihe wa sallam!)
HUMILITY

Note:- The Holy Prophet *(sallallaho alaihe wa sallam!)* was more unassuming than all the people of the world. There are not one or two but thousands of events of his humility, but writers have narrated them in the form of examples.

Once, in a journey, some Companions thought of slaughtering a goat and divided its work also among themselves. One Companion took upon himself the task of slaughtering, one of skinning it, and some of cooking it. The Holy Prophet *(sallallaho alaihe wa sallam!)* offered his own service for collecting fuel for cooking, but the Companions said that they would do this also. So he said: "I also understand that you would do it gladly but neither do I like it nor does Allah like it that I should be more prominent than others in the company."

Hadith 1:- It is reported from Hazrat Umar *(razi Allaho anho!)* that the Holy Prophet *(sallallaho alaihe wa sallam!)* said: "Do not exaggerate in praising me so much as the Christians did in extolling Jesus that they made him Allah's son. I am only Allah's slave. So call me Allah's slave and His apostle".

Note:- The purport of the hadith is that to eulogise a person in such a way that it may smack of polytheism

227

(*shirk*) is not permissible. Praise that may spoil a man's habits must be avoided.

Hadith 2:- It is reported from Hazrat Anas ibn Malik (*razi Allaho anho!*) that a woman came to the Holy Prophet's (*sallallaho alaihe wa sallam!*) presence and said: "I wish to tell you something in private". He said: "Go and sit at some road; I will come there and hear you".

Note:- It appears from some traditions that this woman was somewhat imbecile. Even then he heard her attentively. Some ulema have stated that he asked that woman to sit at roadside for the reason that she was a stranger (not within the prohibited degrees) and some have said that she was demented and so she used to wander on the roads and hence he told her to sit somewhere on the road where he would go and listen to her.

Hadith 3:- It is reported from Hazrat Anas (*razi Allaho anho!*) that the Holy Prophet (*sallallaho alaihe wa sallam!*) used to inquire after the health of the sick, accompany funeral processions, ride donkeys and accept in slaves' invitation. On the day of the fight with Banu Quraizah, he was riding an ass both the rein and saddle of which were made of the bark of date-palm.

Explanation:- The Holy Prophet (*sallallaho alaihe wa sallam!*) when called, would visit any one's house, whether one was rich or poor, a master or a servant, a slave or a slave-woman; and would accept the invitation of every one irrespective of one's status and position. The hauteur, arrogance and snobbery that one notices these days from these he was poles apart. Today the snobs accept an invitation if it comes from wealthy persons, but if it be from a poor family, they make

228

different excuses - of sickness, of business, of going abroad. In sharp contrast to this, the Holy Prophet (*sallallaho alaihe wa sallam!*) would honor every one's invitation. He was in fact so unpretentious and condescending that, according to a tradition recorded by Imam Bukhari, even a slave-woman could catch his hand and lead him to wherever she wanted to take him.

Imam Ahmed has stated that a slave-woman could request him to accompany her for her work. Imam Nasa'i has recorded a tradition that the Holy Prophet (*sallallaho alaihe wa sallam!*) did not feel ashamed of accompanying even a destitute widow, whose need be would try his best to fulfil. Ibn Sa'd has reported that (out of humility) he used to sit on the ground, even eat upon the ground and accept the invitation of even slaves. (*Mawahib-e Ladunniya*, p. 163).

And what is the condition now-a days of those people who claim and pretend to be the servants of the community? There is none to inquire about the wretched plight of the poor, the helpless and the widows; there is none to wipe off their tears; none to lend them money; none to take the trouble of attending the courts for them. These self-styled, self-righteous fame-hungry, pretentious, contemptuous and overly proud servants of society feel ashamed of associating with the down-trodden, the underdog, the poor and the needy whom they, in their private talk, call *hoi polloi*, the scum of society, the rabble. Such haughtiness and thinking scorn of the weaker sections of society is neither liked by Allah nor by His apostle. Allah has had every thing but not humility and helplessness and hence what is valued in His Court is helplessness and humility.

Note:- (1) There used to be a special kind of donkey in Arabia, larger than the Indian mule, and in race it could outrun ponies. Two and even three persons used to rise it. The meaning of the hadith is that, notwithstanding his high rank, which was higher than that of all people, the Holy Prophet (*sallallaho alaihe wa sallam!*) did not consider it below his dignity or degrading to ride a donkey. (2) The Holy Prophet (*sallallaho alaihe wa sallam!*) used to inquire after the health of all sorts of people, whether Muslim or non-Muslim, wicked or virtuous. For instance, he went to inquire after the health of a Jewish boy, who, before his illness, often used to come to him. The boy was on his last legs. So the Holy Prophet (*sallallaho alaihe wa sallam!*) talked to him about accepting Islam. The sick boy looked towards his father and the Jew permitted him to do so. The boy accepted Islam and died a Muslim. The Holy Prophet (*sallallaho alaihe wa sallam!*) thanked Allah that Allah saved the boy through him from the torment of Hell.

The most conspicuous of all such cases is that of Abd Allah ibn Ubbai, the chief of the hypocrites. The noble and large-hearted Prophet (*sallallaho alaihe wa sallam!*) visited him even to inquire after his health in his fatal illness.

Hadith 4:- It is reported from Hazrat Anas bin Malik (*razi Allaho anho!*) that the Noble Prophet (*sallallaho alaihe wa sallam!*) would accept an invitation even if he was invited to partake barley-bread and stale fat.

Hadith 5:- It is reported from Hazrat Ibn Malik (*razi Allaho anho!*) that though, in the sight of the Companions, there was none more beloved than the Holy Prophet (*sallallaho alaihe wa sallam!*), they would not stand up to welcome him because he himself did not like that anyone should stand up to welcome him.

Note:- Abul Waleed ibn Rasheed says that to stand up to welcome a person is of four kinds:-

(1) To stand up for welcoming a proud person is not permissible. (2) It is abominable to stand up to welcome a man if it is feared that such welcome would create pride in him. (3) It is, however, permissible to accord such welcome if it is not likely to create pride in him. (4) It is praiseworthy (mustahab) to stand up for welcoming a man returning from a long journey.

And Imam Nauwavi has stated that to stand up to welcome the ulema is also praiseworthy.

Explanation:- (1) Qazi Iyaz has written that it is an Iranian custom that one may keep sitting while others have to keep standing in his presence. (2) This practice was forbidden for humility's sake. (3) It was forbidden due to mercy and affection for the people because to keep standing is inconvenient. (4) Another reason for forbidding it was the fear of mischief, because showing more respect engenders mischief. (5) In spite of its being permissible, the Holy Prophet (sallallaho alaihe wa sallam!) forbade it for himself, though he had himself stood up to welcome Ikramah ibn Abu Jahl and 'Adi bin Hatim. There is, however, no objection if one stands up to help a coming person or a sick person.

Hazrat Sa'd ibn Mubarak, the chief of the Aws tribe, had been badly wounded from an arrow in the Battle of the Ditch and had become weak. So the Holy Prophet (sallallaho alaihe wa sallam!) ordered the people to stand up to help their chief. Hence, to stand up for

231

helping is permissible. (*Mawahib*, p. 164). The Companions, because of the prophetic Instruction, had stopped the practice of standing up to welcome any one.

Hadith 6:- Hazrat Imam Hasan reports as follows :-

I inquired from my maternal-uncle, Hazrat Hind ibn Abi Halah – he often used to describe the Holy Prophet's (*sallallaho alaihe wa sallam!*) particulars and I was fond of hearing them - and so, on my asking him, he described the Holy Prophet's (*sallallaho alaihe wa sallam!*) features that he was an exalted, highly dignified man, and his face glistened like the full moon; thus he described the whole auspicious appearance.

Hazrat Imam Hasan (*razi Allaho anho!*) further says :-

For a long time I did not talk about this hadith to my younger brother, Hasain, but when I did tell him about it I came to know that he had heard this hadith earlier than me. Not only this that he had heard this hadith from our maternal-uncle but had also known from our father, Hazrat Ali (*razi Allaho anho!*), the Holy Prophet's (*sallallaho alaihe wa sallam!*) manner of going home and coming out of it as well as other manners. Accordingly, Husain said that when he inquired from our father, Hazrat Ali (*razi Allaho anho!*) the Prophetic manner of going home, he said: 'The Holy Prophet (*sallallaho alaihe wa sallam!*) used to divide his time at home into three parts: one part he spent exclusively in devotions to Allah (i.e., prayers, etc.); the second in discharging the dues of his household (i.e., in talking with them and in inquiring about their conditions, etc); and the third he reserved for his own needs (i.e., rest, sleep, etc.). But this personal leisure also he divided into two parts - one for himself and the other for the people. During this second part top-ranking Companions used to visit him and through them different teachings and topics were conveyed to the masses. From these pre-eminent Companions the Holy Prophet (*sallallaho alaihe wa sallam!*) did not keep anything secret (neither about religious matters nor mundane affairs); that is, all sorts of benefits were imparted to them without stint.

As regards this public time the Holy Prophet's (*sallallaho alaihe wa sallam!*) method was that, in admission, he would give preference to men of learning and accomplishments according each time in proportion to the depth and extent of one's learning and knowledge. Such visitors came with one, two or several needs each. He would fulfil all their needs and would engage them in such matters which would be beneficial and useful for themselves as well as for the education and improvement of the whole ummah. For example, after answering the Companions' queries about religious matters, he used to instruct them to convey this knowledge to those people also who were absent due to any reason (women due to purdah, others due to his awe, and still others due to long distance); and he would also ask the visiting Companions to bring to him the needs of such absentees, because, he would say, if a man conveys to the king the need of that person who cannot present it personally, Allah Most High will keep his (conveyor's) steps steadfast on the Day of Judgement, and so he stressed upon the Companions who used to come to him frequently to make efforts in this regard.

Only useful and important matters were discussed in the prophetic majlis. The Holy Prophet (*sallallaho alaihe wa sallam!*) would be glad to hear only about such topics from the Companions. Gossip and newsmongering had no place in his majlis. The Companions used to come to his majlis as seekers of religious knowledge and would not return without having tasted something. (By tasting is meant the acquisition of religious knowledge, but it is also possible that they really partook something, because the Holy Prophet (*sallallaho alaihe wa sallam!*) did offer often whatever pot-luck was present in the house; when close friends are present in a majlis customarily the pot-luck is shared with them).

From the prophetic majlis the Companions used to emerge as the torchbearers of goodness, guidance and knowledge, for the knowledge they imbibed there they used to convey and impart to others; they were truly lode-stars for the ummah.

Imam Husain (*razi Allaho anho!*) reports that when he inquired about the Holy Prophet's (*sallallaho alaihe wa sallam!*) coming out of the house, Hazrat Ali (*razi Allaho anho!*) used to hold his tongue from all things but necessary matters. He would not waste his time in mere chit-chat. He used to win over the hearts of visitors, familiarise them with himself and would not scare them (i.e., in warning them he would not adopt a style which might cause them fright in attending his majlis nor would he describe or discuss such matters which might make them averse to religion). He used to honour and hold in esteem the chief and leader of every tribe and used to appoint him as chief and superintendent of the tribe on his own behalf also. He used to frighten the people with Allah's wrath and punishment and insisted upon them to save themselves from harmful things or to be on their guard in relation to other people, and (as interpreted by Maulana Shaikh al-Hadith Zakariya

234

Sahib) used to save himself too from being harmed or troubled by others.

Note:- The detail regarding this is that to be suspicious of others is not permissible but to be on one's guard and to be wary of others without suspecting is better. The instructions for being chary in relation to others and to do a work after due deliberation are present in a number of traditions.

A factual story is recorded in the *Abu Da'ud* that once the Holy Prophet (*sallallaho alaihe wa sallam!*) thought of sending some goods to Mecca for distribution. He charged this task to a Companion Hazrat Ibnul Faghwa and asked him to find out a companion to accompany him. While ibnul Faghwa was searching for such a man, a man named 'Amr came to him and said: "I have come to know that you are in search of a companion to accompany you to Mecca; I am to go there and so I will accompany you". Ibnul Faghwa came to the Holy Prophet's (*sallallaho alaihe wa sallam!*) presence and said that he had come by a companion who was ready to go to Mecca. When asked who he was, Ibnul Faghwa narrated the whole thing. The Holy Prophet (*sallallaho alaihe wa sallam!*) said: "When you approach the habitation of that man's tribe, be on your guard, for there is a proverb: 'Be wary of your Bekr-brother'! (Bekr is the name of a tribe).

Then, both of us, reports Ibnul Faghwa, set out. When the habitations of my companion's tribe came in sight, he told me: "I will be back in a jiffy after meeting my kith and kin. You please wait for me". "It is of no consequence; go and meet them", said I. But after his going away came to my mind the Holy Prophet's (*sallallaho alaihe wa sallam!*) precious advice and I immediately readied my camel and set off. After some time I saw that he was coming with some men; but being wary, I gave him the slip and slipped off from there hastily.

Explanation:- To entertain suspicion and mistrust about anyone is not permissible; but since a man's religious condition has not been scrutinised, to distrust him in worldly matters, not to deposit any thing with him or through him and not to have too much trust in him are all included in prudence.

A man praised another man before Hazrat Umar Farouq (razi Allaho anho!). Hazrat Umar asked him: "Did you ever entrust a deposit to him? Did you ever lend him monkey or goods? Have you ever tested him"? When he replied in the negative, Hazrat Umar said: "A man is tested and known through such dealings, not by his praying and fasting". Hence the evidence of an unidentified man of obscure circumstances shall not be accepted as long as his circumstances are not examined closely, although his outward appearance may be alright. Similarly the traditionists too have made it a rule that as long as man of obscure condition is not identified, his hadith shall not be accepted. It is for this reason that the Holy Prophet (sallallaho alaihe wa sallam!) has observed: "Keep the love of your friend in the middle path; it is possible that he might become your enemy some time".

That is, if you trust a friend too much and reveal all your private matters and secrets to him, it is just possible that if he becomes your enemy he might inflict harm upon you and bring disgrace to you in the society by divulging your secrets. Prudence, therefore, requires that all the secrets must not be divulged to a friend. To be discreet is not to be suspicious. The Holy Prophet's (*sallallaho alaihe wa sallam!*) story of discretion: He dictated certain instructions in a letter to be sent to the commander of an army and advised him to read it at a particular place and act accordingly (*Bukhari*, vol. i, p.15). That is, if the contents of the letter were to be said orally, the Hypocrites or the intelligencers might have informed the enemy and the purpose for which the Holy Prophet (*sallallaho alaihe wa sallam!*) was dispatching the army would not have been achieved. Hence he got the instructions put on paper and instructed the commander to open it for reading after reaching a certain place and then act as per instructions.

It was an act of the Holy Prophet's (*sallallaho alaihe wa sallam!*) discreetness that rather than get them nabbed and punished, he gave amnesty to the Hypocrites. Had he punished them, the English, American and European orientalists and missionaries, garbling the event would have slung mud at his fair and holy character. Once he sent a batch of Companions to a certain place but there they did not observe discreetness. There they ate dates and unthinkingly threw away the stones. When the enemies stumbled upon fresh date-stones they drew the inference that men must have come from Madina. They launched a search and caught them, and thus the Companions, due to lack of discreetness, were put to loss.

We, the present day Muslims, ought to be all the more circumspect and vigilant because the period in which we are living is fraught with fraud and deceit. Wily tricksters, and wolves in sheep's clothing, making a show of innocence, sympathy and helpfulness easily succeed in putting the simple-minded and the unwary into trouble. It is, therefore, advisable to refrain from trusting strangers, even acquaintances; the frequent cases of cheating and fraud that take place nowadays, particularly during travelling, are mostly due to having too much trust in others.

In short, man can save himself from different religious and worldly losses if he acts according to the said instructions of the Holy Prophet (*sallallaho alaihe wa sallam!*). There goes the adage that the vigilant male is always a happy man'. Similarly, in the matter of religion, too, utmost vigilance and circumspection is a primary need, almost imperative. If a man, considering an unworthy, innovative (*bid'ati*) man to be virtuous, makes him his teacher or spiritual guide (*murshid*), he is sure to ruin his faith (*iman*) and religious life. Hence trust should be placed in people after having tested them according to the sunnah.

The Holy Prophet (*sallallaho alaihe wa sallam!*) used to threaten the people with Allah's punishment (or insist upon them to save themselves from harmful things or to be wary of others) and used to save himself as well from the harm and mischief of the people. Though he was himself wary of others and warned the people also to be on their guard from others, he never allowed wariness to impair his affability and cheerfulness. He used to take care of his friends and, inquiring into the conditions and mutual relations of the people, used to improve them; praising a good act, he used to encourage it, and showing the evil of a bad work, he used to discourage it and prevent the people from doing it again.

In every thing the Holy Prophet (*sallallaho alaihe wa sallam!*) used to adopt the golden mean, scrupulously avoiding fickleness and confused thinking - saying one thing now and another at another time. He was never inattentive in reforming and improving the people lest they became unheeding towards religion or weary of it due to exceeding the limit in any religious matter. With him every work had a particular method. In respect of divine orders he neither showed remissness nor ever exceeded the limits. Those who used to frequent his majlis were the noblest individuals, the cream of society, but the most superior amongst them in his eyes was one whose fellow-feeling was catholic (i.e., one who wished well for all). The high-ranking in his sight used to be one who took greater part in sympathising with and helping the people.

Hazrat Imam Husain (*razi Allaho anho!*) reports that when he inquired about Holy Prophet's (*sallallaho alaihe wa sallam!*) majlis, Hazrat Ali (*razi Allaho anho!*) said: His sitting down and standing up both used to be with the remembrance of Allah. Whenever he went anywhere he would sit down wherever he found a seat and used to instruct the people also to sit wherever they found place for sitting and refrain from leaping over others' heads to go ahead. It is a different thing that wherever he sat down, that place used to become the main seat of the majlis. He used to discharge the right of every individual in the audience; i.e., as regards cheerfulness and conversation, he would fulfil the due right of every one so that each man in the audience used to think that the Holy Prophet (*sallallaho alaihe wc sallam!*) was treating him with more attention and favour.

Anyone who sat with him or came to consult him in any matter, the Holy Prophet (*sallallaho alaihe wa sallam!*) would keep sitting with him until the visitor himself rose up. If anyone demanded anything from him,

239

he would give to him and if the demanded thing was not available, he would give a polite answer. His affability and cheerfulness were common for all. As regards affection, he was the father of all the people and in respect of rights all the people were equal in his eyes. His majlis used to be an assembly of knowledge and modesty, patience and trust (amanat); i.e., these four characteristics were always present in his majlis. There would be neither din and noise nor calumny and vilification for anyone; if someone ever committed an error in the majlis; it was never given publicity to. Mutually all were considered equal (irrespective of their lineage) but there used to be superiority over each other by virtue of one's piety. Every one behaved with each other, treating the elders with respect and showing affection to the young; and they all gave preference to the needy and looked after the traveller.

Note:- In short, every thing and every work was on an ideal plane, higher than the highest degree of excellent morals. And why should it not be when the Holy Prophet's (sallallaho alaihe wa sallam!) commission itself was meant to perfect the morals? Although his excellent morals have been mentioned in the holy Quran and Allah Most Glorious has described his ideal morality and virtues with various degrees of emphasis, he often used to pray: "O Allah! Even as You have endowed me with good looks, invest me with elegant morals also"! One of his statements is: Allah Most High likes soft heartedness and awards that much for softness of heart which He does not award for anything else. It says in one hadith that a man lacking mildness lacks a great good. One hadith says: "The best person amongst you is one whose morals are best." It says in another hadith: "Dearer to me amongst you is the person whose morals are good." A Companion asked the

Holy Prophet (*sallallaho alaihe wa sallam!*): "What is the best thing that has been bestowed upon man"? "Good disposition," said he. "On the Day of Judgement", says one hadith, "the weightiest thing in the Balance of the Book of Deeds will be good morals." The prophetic statement in one hadith is that "through good morals one can attain the rank of that man who keeps vigil at night and fasts during day." Hazrat Mo'az (*razi Allaho anho!*) reports that when he was being sent to Yemen and he put his foot into the stirrup to ride, the last advice the Holy Prophet (*sallallaho alaihe wa sallam!*) gave him was: "Behave good-humouredly with the people". One prophetic statement is that "amongst the believers the men of most perfect faith (*iman*) are those whose morals are good".

There are numerous such hadiths in which good morals have been emphasised for cultivation; the one quoted above are only a sample thereof.

* * * * * * * *

LVII

SUMMARY

PROPOSITIONS DERIVED FROM THE SAID HADITHS

It is permissible to hide a point of knowledge from a brother or friend due to some reason.

(2) It is permissible to inquire about a proposition (*mas'ala*) from several persons.

(3) A neat schedule of engagements and works occupying all the 24 hours makes for convenience and also benefits the visitors. This method is seen in actual practice at the places of saints. There everything is done on schedule, for there is a scheduled time for each activity: for teaching and giving lessons, for writing, for giving amulets to the needy, for meals, for tea, for meeting visitors, etc. The whole programme becomes easy by following the said hadith and each work can be accomplished in time. Through Allah's grace and kindness, whatever I am offering to the readers is due to such division of time.

(4) It is permissible to fix a time for discharging the rights of the wife and the children.

(5) It is permissible that one may not talk before common people on topics one may talk before particular men.

(6) In social intercourse and meeting people it is an act of sunnah to behave according to the ability and capacity of the people.

(7) One should try to engage the services of disciples and pupils in the ummah's work.

(8) Particular persons should be made responsible to convey important propositions and topics to the masses.

(9) It is a social duty to convey the needs of the public to the ruler and to extend help and cooperation to him as per one's capacity in their fulfillment.

(10) The feet of the conveyor of public needs to the ruler will not stagger on the Day of Judgement.

(11) Necessary and useful academic talk should be given in public gatherings.

(12) Important and useful talks should be heard attentively.

(13) It is necessary to avoid useless, frivolous talk in a majlis, for it would be a sheer waste of time, both yours and others.

(14) A seeker of knowledge will surely benefit if he goes respectfully to the majlis of the ulema, the virtuous, and the saints. The well-to-do and wealthy merchants and business-magnates call upon the ulema just to overawe them; this is abominable (*makruh*). The managing and running of mosques and madrasahs on commercial basis is causing the baraka (prosperity) to vanish.

(15) When a man comes as a seeker of knowledge to a majlis of the ulema, they should make him taste knowledge and give him some appropriate advice.

(16) The visiting guests should be dined as per one's capacity.

(17) The noble Companions used to carry guidance from the Holy Prophet's (*sallaho alaihe wa sallam!*) majlis to the masses. This alone is called *tabligh* (preaching) for which the ummah has been made responsible.

(18) It is necessary to save the tongue from frivolous talk.

(19) Whether the visitors are guests or students, it is necessary to show kindness to them; they must not be frightened lest they become averse to knowledge and religion.

(20) The chief, leader or ruler of every community and clan should be respected.

(21) A post should be assigned to one in accordance with one's ability.

(22) One should always observe vigilance and discrectness in every work.

(23) To be always cheerful and to meet everyone cheerfully is an act of sunnah.

(24) It is also an act of sunnah to behave in a civil manner with all.

(25) To remain in touch with the conditions of friends and relatives so that they may not digress from the right path and to explain to them if there is anything needing correction, is a religious responsibility.

(26) To adopt the golden mean in every work is a sunnah.

(27) Those who cherished sympathy and kindly feelings for the community had great value in the Holy Prophet's (*sallallaho alaihe wa sallam!*) eyes.

(28) It is an act of sunnah to remember Allah while sitting down and standing up - in fact in every posture.

(29) In a function or majlis one should seat oneself wherever one can find a vacant place and should avoid leaping over the necks of others unnecessarily.

(30) All should be treated equally; it is particularly necessary for a teacher to treat all students equally. Discriminative treatment and unequal distribution of favours ("plum cakes to some and oil-cakes to others") are damaging to the honour of a king, master, teacher, manager, secretary etc.

(31) The right of every one in the audience ought to be discharged.

(32) A man who comes and sits in the majlis should be shown kindness.

(33) Excellence is due to piety, not due to riches and high post, but in the present society excellence is deemed to consist in affluence and influence.

(34) If some one commits a fault in the majlis, it must not be publicised.

(35) It is necessary to refrain from recrimination and the creation of din and noise.

(36) The elders should be shown respect, the young affection.

(37) The needs of the needy ought to be fulfilled.

(38) If a traveller or stranger happens to come to the majlis and has any urgent need or work, he should be helped after due enquiry of his circumstances.

Ponder over it. What a beautiful picture of the prophetic morals emerges from this hadith every sentence of which establishes a proposition. It is because of this meaningfulness of this hadith that I have drawn your attention to it; the more one reads it minutely the more one can draw legal (*shar'ai*) orders and moral lessons.

Alas! the lesson the Great Prophet (*sallallaho alaihe wa sallam!*) imparted to us, we, through our folly and lack of appreciation, consigned to oblivion and consequently degenerated. May Allah help us!

Hadith 7:- It is reported by Hazrat Anas ibn Malik (*razi Allaho anho!*) that a tailor invited the Holy Prophet (*sallallaho alaihe wa sallam!*) for dining. The food was *tharid*, having pieces of pumpkin in it. Since the Holy Prophet (*sallallaho alaihe wa sallam!*) liked pumpkin much, he began to eat its pieces.

"Thereafter", says Hazrat Anas about himself, "no food was prepared for me in which I could afford to add white pumpkin and it might not have been added".

Note:- *Tharid* is a dish consisting of soup in which pieces of bread are immersed. Some scholars have translated *dobba* as white pumpkin while some say it is pumpkin. However, the ulema have stated that to eat white pumpkin is a sunnah.

Hadith 8:- Hazrat 'Amrah bint Abd al-Rehman (*ibn Sa'd bin Zararah*) reports that someone asked Hazrat Ayesha (*razi Allaho anha!*): "What did the Holy Prophet (*sallallaho alaihe wa sallam!*) do at home"? She said: "He was also a man like other men. He used to search out lice from his clothes, milk goats and do his own works personally".

Note:- It is evident from this hadith that the Holy Prophet (*sallallaho alaihe wa sallam!*) did not consider it below his dignity to do his own works. Other hadiths also corroborate it that he would patch his own clothes, sweep the floor of the house and carry articles home from the bazar personally.

Explanation:- As regards this hadith that mentions the seeking out of lice from the clothes, the ulema have explained that there used to be no lice on his body or in his clothes, for lice, they say, breed due to filthiness and perspiration, whereas he was all light and hence there arises no question of filthiness, and his perspiration was as good as rosewater which people used as perfume. The fact is, as the ulema have proved convincingly, that he used to search for those lice that might have climbed his clothes from the filthy clothes of others, particularly of the desert-Arabs with whom he used to come in contact freely; the very practice of removing lice from the clothes and the attention paid to this work shows how careful he was about personal cleanliness. Besides this, by his own example he wanted to teach the slovenly among the fellow-Arabs to cultivate a sense of hygiene and cleanliness.

Explanation:- Humility and slavehood ('abadiyat) – self-effacement and self-renunciation – were the outstanding characteristics of the Holy Prophet (*sallallaho alaihe wa sallam!*). He was poles apart from a life of vanity and superciliousness and always insisted upon the people to remain away from these things, because Allah likes humility, submissiveness and self-effacement most.

It is for this reason that he observed: "In no other phase of prayer is man nearer to Allah than in prostration". And it was again for this reason that when Allah Most High described the Holy Prophet's (*sallallaho dlaihe wa sallam!*) great journey from the Masjid-e Haram to the Masjid-e Aqsa, He used the word 'slave' for him: The Holy Being transported His slave ('abd) from the Haram Mosque to the Aqsa Mosque in a certain part of night (Quran). It appears from this that in the Court of Allah no other thing is as much valued and appreciated as an 'abd. It was because of this knowledge that the Holy Prophet (*sallallaho alaihe wa sallam!*), in spite of being a great apostle, the Seal of the Prophet, used to do all his works himself. If his Companions, during a journey, divided any work among themselves, he too would share and participate in that work. In making his own bed, repairing his broken chappal, etc as well as in the matter of clothes and conveyance, he had adopted a life of humility and self-effacement.

LVIII

THE HOLY PROPHET'S
(*sallallaho alaihe wa sallam!*)
MORALS & CIVIL MORES

The Holy Prophet's (*sallallaho alaihe wa sallam!*) noble habits and excellent morals are proverbial throughout the world; the fame of Muhammadi morals is phenomenal and universal. What can be greater than this that Allah Most Glorious Himself hath eulogised him in the holy Quran and hath observed in the *Sura-e Nun: "Innaka la'ala khulqin azim"* ("Lo! thou art of a tremendous nature")? With what great emphasis hath the Lord Most High said in this verse that "verily, you possess great morals".

To compute and totalise all his excellent morals is a difficult task. A large portion of the tomes of Hadith is comprised of those hadiths only that describe his morals but here only a few of them are reproduced as sample.

Hadith 1:- It is reported that a group of people went to Hazrat Zaid ibn Thabit (*razi Allaho anho!*) and requested him to describe before them the Holy Prophet's (*sallallaho alaihe wa sallam!*) morals. He (Zaid) said: "What particulars may I tell you (i.e., it is difficult to narrate all). Know that I was his neighbour (i.e., I was often present near him and know many of his conditions) and was also his amanuensis, transcribing the divine revelations. Whenever any divine revelation came to him, he used to call me. I would attend him and write down the revelation. (He used to be very informal and kindly with us). He would talk with us about the same things we talked about; if we talked about worldly affairs, he too would talk about them (and not that he would always talk about the Hereafter, disliking the mundane topics).

And when we paid attention towards the Hereafter, he also described the things thereof; i.e., if a topic concerning the Hereafter was broached, then he too would narrate its particulars and details; and when we indulged in talking about food and drink, he also took part in such talk describing the etiquette of eating and drinking, its advantages, the names of delicious foods and the kinds of harmful ones, etc.

Note:- The topics touched in this hadith have been elucidated a little along with its translation. Shaikh al-Hadith Maulana Zakariya Sahib says that Hazrat Zaid's statement that "What particulars may I tell you" means that he (Zaid) could describe every condition of the Holy Prophet (*sallallaho alaihe wa sallam!*) and so could tell them whatever they wanted to hear as he was the Holy Prophet's (*sallallaho alaihe wa sallam!*) neighbour as well as amanuensis. The Holy Prophet's (*sallallaho alaihe wa sallam!*) conditions included particulars regarding both the religion and the world, eating and drinking, in fact, every aspect of life. And so Zaid was in two minds as to which aspect he should describe, for each description was wonderful and every condition exquisite and interesting.

Hazrat Zaid's statement in this hadith that he was summoned at the time of divine revelation is that he was mostly present amongst the amanuenses of hadith counted the following persons also : Hazrat Usman, Hazrat Ali, Hazrat Amir Mua'wiya, Hazrat Khalid ibn

250

sa'eed, Hazrat Hanzalah, Hazrat 'Ala al-Hazrami, Hazrat Abban ibn Sa'eed and Hazrat Ubby ibn Ka'b.

A question arises from the said hadith that the mention of food and drink is quite useless and meaningless because it is stated in a hadith that the Holy Prophet (sallallaho alaihe wa sallam!) used to save his auspicious tongue from useless talk. So why was a useless talk about eating and drinking mentioned here? The answer to this question is that the mention of every worldly thing is not useless. On the contrary, talking about the worldly affairs and particularly regarding food and drink was necessary, rather indispensable, for him for the reason that one could know the permissible and the impermissible, the legitimate (halal) and the prohibited (haram), the good and the bad amongst the victuals from his statements only. Accordingly, this topic was also mentioned in the same hadith that the Holy Prophet (sallallaho alaihe wa sallam!), after enquiring about the conditions of the people, used to praise a good thing and show the evil of a bad one. With this purpose in view, worldly matters too were discussed in the prophetic majlis, but none indulged in idle talk.

Hadith 2:- Hazrat 'Amr ibn 'Aas (razi Allaho anho!) reports that the Holy Prophet (sallallaho alaihe wa sallam!), in his special talk, used to pay attention even to the worst man in the community with a view to win his heart. "Towards me also", states 'Amr, "he used to pay much attention, addressing me more than he did others, wherefore I began to think that I was the best man in the community. So under this impression, one day I asked him: "Sir, am I superior or Abu Bakr'? 'Abu Bakr', he replied. Then I asked: 'Am I superior or Umar'? He said, 'Umar'. Again I asked: 'Am I superior or Usman'? He replied: 'Usman'. When I asked him clearly, he told

251

me correctly, without fear or favour, and later on I thought that I should not have asked him such things."

Note:- 'Amr ibn 'Aas (*razi Allaho anho!*) used to consider himself superior to all due to the Holy Prophet's (*sallallaho alaihe wa sallam!*) special attention. From a long hadith in the foregone it has already been known that the Holy Prophet's (*sallallaho alaihe wa sallam!*) noble habit was to give preference in showing courtesy, so much so that, for the sake of conciliation, even infidels and Hypocrites were treated with attention.

The said order of personalities in the above-mentioned questioning is due to the fact that in the Holy Prophet's (*sallallaho alaihe wa sallam!*) lifetime itself the Companions used to consider Hazrat Abu Bakr (*razi Allaho anho!*) to be the most superior person. Accordingly it is clearly mentioned in other hadiths that "in the Holy Prophet's (*sallallaho alaihe wa sallam!*) lifetime itself we used to consider Hazrat Abu Bakr and then Hazrat Umar and then Hazrat Usman to be the most superior persons". That is, the superiority and excellence of all the three was so explicit during the Holy Prophet's (*sallallaho alaihe wa sallam!*) life itself that all the Companions used to acknowledge it.

Hazrat Ali's son Muhammad asked him as to who was the most superior person next to the Holy Prophet (*sallallaho alaihe wa sallam!*). He said: "Abu Bakr". Then he asked again: "Who next"? He said: "Umar". Besides this there are a number of hadiths that describe the same order.

Meaning of Mudarat :

To spend wealth for defending religion, to behave well, to expend money for saving oneself from the enemies, all these actions are included in mudarat (courtesy) and all such actions are permissible.

Meaning of Mudahat :

Mudahat (hypocrisy) consists in ruining the religion for the sake of the world. There are Muslims today who, in order to obtain a ticket for election to the Local Board, Legislative Assembly or Parliament, do not hesitate to give statements against Islam, against the religious practices against the Muslim personal law or against the Islamic institution of polygamy. This mudahat (hypocrisy) is haram (prohibited). Anyone who speaks against Islam automatically goes out of the pale of Islam. Such Muslims are like the Hypocrites; under the cover and in the name of Islam they grind their own axe and try to obtain their mess of pottage. People should keep from such Muslims rather shun them completely.

* * * * * *

LIX

THE HOLY PROPHET'S
(Sallallaho alaihe wa sallam!)
BASHFULNESS & MODESTY

Note:- Incidents showing the Holy Prophet's *(sallallaho alaihe wa sallam!)* modesty are not one or two; they are legion, but only a few are reproduced here as a specimen.

Hazrat Ibn Umar *(razi Allaho anho!)* reports that Holy Prophet *(sallallaho alaihe wa sallam!)*, due to utmost bashfulness, would never fix his gaze at anyone's face; i.e., he never stared at anyone.

Hadith 1:- Hazrat Abu Sa'eed Khudri *(razi Allaho anho!)* reports that the Holy Prophet *(sallallaho alaihe wa sallam!)*, in modesty and bashfulness, surpassed a virgin who may be behind the purdah. "If he disliked anything, we used to recognise it from his face; due to excessive modesty, he did not like to express his dislike."

Note:- The ulema have stated two meanings of "the virgin who may be behind the purdah" (1) One group of scholars says that by it is meant that purdah-observing virgin who is usually more bashful than a virgin goes here and there without purdah, though every virgin is more or less bashful. It is for this reason that the Shari'ah has called a virgin's silence sufficient as consent for her nikah.

(2) The second meaning is that by it is meant that girl who may have been reared in purdah and may have observed purdah even from other women. It is then obvious that such a virgin must be much more bashful than those who go about without purdah.

Hadith 2:- Hazrat Ayesha (*razi Allaho anha!*) reports that due to the Holy Prophet's (*sallallaho alaihe wa sallam!*) bashfulness she could never dare to look or ever looked at his private parts.

Note:- When due to his bashfulness she could not muster courage to see, how he too could have seen, for it is a matter of principle that one has to behave bashfully before a bashful person. It is clearly mentioned in another tradition that neither the Holy Prophet (*sallallaho alaihe wa sallam!*) ever saw her private parts nor she his. And when Hazrat Ayesha's (*razi Allaho anha!*) condition be such, though she was much more frank and most beloved amongst all the holy wives, what can be said of other wives? Hazrat Salmah (*razi Allaho anha!*) reports that the Holy Prophet (*sallallaho alaihe wa sallam!*) used to close his eyes and bend his head during the sexual congress and also insisted upon the wife to be dignified and quiet. It is stated in Hazrat Ibn Abbas's tradition that the Holy Prophet (*sallallaho alaihe wa sallam!*) used to go behind the room to take bath and no one ever saw his covered parts.

* * * * * *

255

LXI

THE HOLY PROPHET'S
(Sallallaho alaihe wa sallam!)
RESORTING TO CUPPING

The word *'hajamat'* in this chapter means cupping; i.e., to draw blood from the affected part of the body by means of a cupping-glass which is a horn-shaped instrument with a small hole at its tapering and. In the olden times the cuppers used to have horns of deer for this purpose. It is an ancient remedial method in which small cuts or snicks are made with a sharp razor on the aching part of the body and then the broad opening of the horn or cupping-glass is placed on the affected, snicked portion and the cupper, taking the tapering end in his own mouth, starts sucking the impure blood. Thereafter he applies some medicine or salve to the snicked portion to stop the oozing of blood, relieve pain and heal the wounds.

Note:- This method was in vogue not only in the ancient times and the middle ages but was also in use in the modern period. (Once in a blue moon though, even now one comes across the practitioner of this near-obsolete ancient art. Translator). The Holy Prophet's *(sallallaho alaihe wa sallam!)* resorting to this method for the cure of certain bodily ailments shows that it was his practice to avail of the current medical therapy whenever necessary, for any remedial action is not contrary to trust in Allah. Who could have had greater trust in Allah than him? Even so he did have resort to this prevailing method as a remedy, and the truth is that the making use of means is not contrary to trust in Allah (tawakkul).

Shah Vali Allah Deh* lvi, in one of his treatises in which he has described the questions he put to the Holy Prophet (sallallaho alaihe wa sallam!) in dreams, writes that "once I put a spiritual question to him whether it was superior to adopt the means or renounce them, and from him I received a spiritual grace (fayz), whereby my heart turned lukewarm towards means, children and every thing else. Thereafter a mystery became exposed intuitively to my mind that while the disposition turns towards means, the soul is inclined towards resignation and confiding (to Allah). (The sum and substance of this statement is that the adoption of means is not contrary to trust in Allah).

Explanation:- To adopt means and to act and then have trust in Allah - this is tawakul; to believe the means or causes to be effective and to consider them to be everything can be the cause of and lead one to apostasy.

Hadith 1:- Hazrat Anas (razi Allaho anho!) reports that someone asked him the proposition whether it was permissible or not to charge the fees for cupping; and he replied that Abu Taiba had cupped the Holy Prophet (sallallaho alaihe wa sallam!) and his holiness and paid him two sa's (a measure) of eatables (according to another tradition, two sa's of dates), and through recommendation to Abū Taiba's masters had also got the tax (payable by him) reduced; and also stated that "cupping is the best remedy".

Note:- When the Holy Prophet (sallallaho alaihe wa sallam!) himself paid the remuneration for cupping, the answer to the said query is quite clear: that to charge its

257

fees is permissible. The purpose of asking this proposition was possibly this that in certain hadiths the profession of cupping has been run down (and so the said query was made). The purpose of depreciating this profession is this that the cupper has to suck impure blood from the affected part of the body through the cupping glass and blood is an unclean thing, let alone the possibility of the cupper's catching a disease himself. The cupper, therefore, must be very careful in sucking the blood, of course, he does not guip it but spits it out, but he must rinse his mouth thoroughly after the operation. (If he takes this care, then there is no objection against practising this profession).

* * * * * * *

LXI

THE HOLY PROPHET'S
(Sallallaho alaihe wa sallam!)
NAMES AND TITLES

In view of the Holy Prophet's *(sallallaho alaihe wa sallam!)* praises and honour, many honorific names and titles have been used and described. As many as one thousand names have been reproduced from Ibnul Arabi in the commentary of the *Tirmizi*. In his own book, Allamah Suyuti has stated five hundred names.

Particular names have been mentioned in the hadiths on particular occasions but all these names have not been encompassed in a single tradition.

It says in one hadith that "seven names have been used for me in the holy Quran: (1) Muhammad. (2) Ahmed, (3) Yasin, (4) Ta Ha, (5) Mudaththir, (6) Muzzammil, (7) Abd Allah."

The excess of names is usually indicative of nobleness and honour.

Hadith 1:- Hazrat Jubayr ibn Mut'im reports that the Holy Prophet *(sallallaho alaihe wa sallam!)* said: "There are many names of mine. Among them are Muhammad and Ahmed and Mabi, which means 'the obliterator', for Allah Most High hath obliterated kufr (infidelity) through me; l and one name is Hashir (for on the Day of Judgement. Allah Most High will raise me first of all and the entire ummah will be raised after me and thus I will be the cause of the resurrection of the whole ummah). And one name of mine is 'Aaqib ('the successor', for I came after all the prophets and now there will be no prophet after me)".

Note:- The ulema have said that the name 'Muhammad' is his proper name, peculiar to him only, for no one among the earlier peoples ever took this name. However, when the time of his birth drew near, many people named their sons Muhammad in the hope that some offspring of theirs might deserve the glad tidings prophesied in the earlier Books and might turn out to be a prophet; but Allah knoweth better the place where He proposes to bestow His apostlehood.

Hadith 2:- Hazrat Huzaifa reports that once he came across the Holy Prophet (*sallallaho alaihe wa sallam!*) who was going somewhere. In their talk the Holy Prophet (*sallallaho alaihe wa sallam!*) said: "My name is Muhammad and also Ahmed, and Nabi al-Rahmat and Nabi al-Tawba, and I am Maqaffi and Hashir and Nabi al-Malahim".

Note:- These names were specially mentioned because these were written in the earlier Books by way of prophesy of his advent, and the scripturaries (Ahl-e Kitab) used to recognise him with these names and attributes.

The name 'Maqaffi' means one who comes last or one who follows the earlier prophets because all the prophets were concordant as regards the essentials of religion. viz., Divine Unity and good morals. 'Nabi al-Malahim' means "the prophet of holy wars". The ummah of no other prophet had to wage so many jihads. Jihad will always remain with this ummah and the last will be waged against the Anti-Christ. The word 'mulhima' also means collectivity, congregation, assemblage and the healing of the wound. The collectivism that was characteristic of the Islamic ummah and is still found in this degenerated state in spite of differences is not to be found continuously in the ummah of any another prophet. 'Mulhima' also means 'a tremendous tumult'. Before the approach of the Doomsday the will crop up extremely horrible disturbances in this ummah, like that of the Anti-Christ. Every prophet from Prophet Noah onwards has prophesied and warned about the coming of the Anti-Christ and his mischief-making. Similarly, there will be other terrible disorders and anarchy like that of the Gog and Magog the portents of which have already begun to appear.

* * * * * *

LXII

THE HOLY PROPHET
(*sallallaho alaihe wa sallam!*)
LIVELIHOOD

Note:- From the beginning to its end the Holy Prophet (*sallallaho alaihe wa sallam!*) life, in spite of the coming of wealth which was spent in charities, was a life of poverty and hunger. In fact the pleasure that he had in this life of poverty chosen by himself is simply indescribable. He has himself stated that Allah Almighty had told him to transmute the land of Mecca into gold for him, but he said: Not this, O Allah! On the contrary, I want to eat to my fill one day so that I may thank You and one day I may remain hungry so that I may implore humbly before You".

The prophetic statement is: "I am not afraid of poverty and starvation for you but I am afraid of this that the world may expand for you even as it had expanded for the people before you, and you may attach your hearts to it as those people had attached and it may annihilate you as it annihilated those people". It is for this reason that at one place the Holy Prophet (*sallallaho alaihe wa sallam!*) has invoked: "O Allah! Fix the livelihood of Muhammad's descendants only that much that may suffice for their needs"! (*Mishkat*).

Hadith 1:- Hazrat Nau man ibn Basheer (*razi Allaho anho!*) says: "Aren't you engrossed in eating and drinking as per your will and desire (and don't you eat as much as you want to) although I have seen the Holy Prophet

262

(*sallallaho alaihe wa sallam!*) that he did not have even third-rate dates for eating to his fill"?

Hadith 2:- Reports Hazrat Ayesha Siddiqa (*razi Allaho anha!*):- "At our home, that is, the home of the Holy Prophet's (*sallallaho alaihe wa sallam!*) household, fire would not be kindled (sometimes) for a month on stretch; we subsisted merely or water and dates".

Note:- The meaning of 'fire would not be kindled' is that there used to be nothing in the house to cook for which the hearth would be kindled. The ulema have stated that the mention of water along with dates is for the reason that even dates were not available in sufficient quantity so as to fill the stomach, and hunger had to be assuaged with a few dates which we washed down with water.

It says in one hadith that complete two months would pass and the new moon of the third would be seen and even then fire would not be kindled in anyone of the Holy Prophet's (*sallallaho alaihe wa sallam!*) houses. Hazrat Ayesha's sister's son, Orwah, asked her: "Dear aunt! then how did you subsist"? "On dates and water", she replied. "However, there were some neighbours from amongst the Ansar who owned milch animals. If someone from amongst them offered milk as a present, we too were given a share from it for drinking", she added.

It is reported in one hadith that once Hazrat Abu Bakr (*razi Allaho anho!*) presented a leg of goat. It was night and Hazrat Ayesha (*razo Allaho anha!*) began to cut it into pieces. Someone asked: "Is there no lamp in the house"? She replied: "Had there been oil for the lamp, wouldn't we have used it for eating"?

The ulema have stated the Holy Prophet (*sallallaho alaihe wa sallam!*) approved this condition for himself and his household although the keys of the treasures of the earth had been offered to him. Thereafter the ummah came to be divided into four groups:-

(1) One group of people consisted of those who did not incline themselves towards the world nor the world inclined towards them, e.g., Hazrat Abu Bakr Siddiq (razi Allah anho!).

(2) The second group consisted of those who did not incline towards the world but the world inclined towards them, e.g., Hazrat Umar Farouq (*razi Allaho anho!*).

(3) The third group comprised of those who inclined towards the world and the world too inclined towards them; e.g., the kings of the Banu Umayyah - with the sole exception of Hazrat Umar bin *Abd* al-Aziz.

(4) The fourth group was made up of those people who inclined towards the world but the world did not incline towards them; e.g., the people whom Allah made fakirs but the love of the world settled in their hearts.

Hadith 3:- Hazrat Abu Talha (*razi Allaho anho!*) reports: we complained to the Holy Prophet (*sallallaho alaihe wa sallam!*) of our keen hunger and showed him the stones tied on our bellies - a stone was tied over the belly of each one of us due to the keenness of hunger. The Holy Prophet (*sallallaho alaihe wa sallam!*) showed us two stones tied to his own stomach, for his hunger was keener than ours as he had passed a longer time than we had without eating."

Note:- It was the habit of the Madinans that when intense hunger rendered them weak and helpless, they used to tie stones on their stomachs so that the buttress of stone would help them walk straight. Even today, when the hunger is very intense, a thick cloth is tied tightly over the stomach as it helps curb the pangs of hunger.

Some ulema say that flatulence is caused in an empty stomach and by tying some hard substance of stone, one is saved from it. Or they used to tie a stone called Mushbe'ah, which is found in Arabia and is said to appease hunger.

Other ulema have written that when the stomach is empty, there is fear of the intestines slipping down. If the stomach is tied, they remain in their natural position and hence they used to tie stones on the empty stomachs.

* * * * * * *

LXIII

THE HOLY PROPHET'S
(*Sallallaho alaihe wa sallam!*)
AUSPICIOUS AGE

Note:- Three kinds of traditions have been reported regarding the Holy Prophet's (*sallallaho alaihe wa sallam!*) auspicious age.

(1) According to the majority of traditionists and historians the most preferable tradition is that which mentions the auspicious age to be sixty-three years.

(2) In another tradition the age mentioned is sixty years about which it is said that while counting the fraction is usually omitted. For example if one is born in the sixth month of 1977, we may omit to mention half of the year 1977.

(3) In the third kind of tradition the age shown is sixty-five years in which the years of birth and death have also been included in counting.

Hadith 1:- Hazrat Ibn Abbas (razi Allho anho!) reports that the Holy Prophet (*sallallaho alaihe wa sallam!*) after receiving prophethood, lived thirteen years in Mecca and during these thirteen years divine revelations continued to come to him; thereafter he emigrated from Mecca and lived in Madina for ten years and then passed away at the age of sixty-three years.

LXIV

REGARDING THE HOLY PROPHET'S
(*Sallallaho alaihe wa sallam!*)
DEMISE

Hadith 1 :- Hazrat Anas (*razi Allaho anho!*) reports (as follows) :-

"The last view of the Holy Prophet (*sallallaho alaihe wa sallam!*) that I had was at a time when in his fatal sickness, at the time of Fajr prayer on Monday, he lifted the curtain of his house in order to have a look at the prayer of his followers for the last time; his countenance, in clearness, lustre and sheen, was like a neat and holy page of the Quran. At that hour the people were saying the Fajr prayer behind Abu Bakr Siddiq. The Companions, seeing the Holy Prophet (*sallallaho alaihe wa sallam!*), began to fall back through excess of joy, thinking that he might join them in prayer, but with a gesticulation he asked them to remain where they were. On the same day he went to glory".

Note:- It is the same scene of Monday from which the Holy Prophet (*sallallaho alaihe wa sallam!*), ascertained that the legal religious order had been fully established and the old, faithful friend, Abu Bakr, would discharge the right and duty of vicegerency properly and would bear the ummah's burden satisfactorily. And it did transpire accordingly which the whole world witnessed that the most sorrowful and heart-breaking incident of the Holy Prophet's (*sallallaho alaihe wa sallam!*) passing away - vis-a-vis which all the calamities and misfortunes were nothing - was coupled with the sedition of apostasy and confrontation with the mightiest powers of the time; and yet that mountain of fortitude and resolution (Hazrat Abu Bakr) held up under the brunt rock-like and shattered to pieces every thing that came into clash with him. The truth is that he discharged the dues of vicegerency most ably and intrepidly. At that time a column of Islam like Harat Umar, who was held in awe by friends and foes alike for his prowess, stout heartedness and strength, had to request Hazrat Abu Bakr to show leniency and had to hear the taunt of timidity.

Hadith 2:- Hazrat Ayesha (*razi Allaho anha!*) reports (as follows):-

"At the time of death while I was supporting the Holy Prophet (*sallallaho alaihe wa sallam!*) against my breast, he sent for a urinal, eased himself and then breathed his last".

Hadith 3:- Hazrat Ayesha (Irazi Allaho anha!) reports (as follows):- "At the time of his demise I had put a bowl of water near the Holy Prophet (*sallallaho alaihe wa sallam!*) in which he was dipping his hands again and again and was drawing them over his auspicious face, and the same time involving Allah: "O Allah! Help me in the agonies of death"!

Note:- In the agony of death when the soul is being separated from the body, the feeling of pang is but natural. At such a time of pain and stress too the Holy Prophet (*sallallaho alaihe wa sallam!*) invokes Allah for ease in dying, which bears in it a lesson for the ummah.

Hadith 4:- Hazrat Ayesha (Irazi Allaho anha!) reports (as follows):-

"After having witnessed the Holy Prophet's (*sallallaho alaihe wa sallam!*) served agony of death, now I don't envy the absence of agony in anyone's fatal sickness".

Explanation:- The easy separator and departure of the soul from the body is no proof of one's popularity in the divine court. Had it been a sign of popularity, the Holy Prophet's (*sallallaho alaihe wa sallam!*) soul would have left the body much more easily, but even he had to suffer the agony of death.

Hadith 5:- Hazrat Ayesha (Irazi Allaho anha!) reports that at the time of the Holy Prophet's (*sallallaho alaihe wa sallam!*) death there occurred difference of opinion among his Companions with regard to his burial. (Some Companions selected the Prophet's Mosque, some chose Baq'ee in view of proximity to his Companions, some were in favour of taking his body to the tomb of his highest ancestor, Prophet Abraham, while still others were thinking of bringing him back to his native-place Mecca). Hazrat Abu Bakr*(razi Allaho anho!)* (hearing the different opinions) said: "I have myself heard one thing from the Holy Prophet (*sallallaho alaihe wa sallam!*) which I remember very well that prophets die at that place only where they like to be buried, and, therefore, he should be buried only at the site of his death".

Note:- After the Holy Prophet's (*sallallaho alaihe wa sallam!*) passing away, since all such matters were to be accomplished at Hazrat Abu Bakr's hands, he was particularly well aware of such propositions.

Hadith 6:- Hazrat Ibn Abbas (*razi Allaho anho!*) and Hazrat Ayesha (*razi Allaho anha!*) report that Hazrat Abu Bakr (*razi Allaho anho!*) came after the Holy Prophet's (*sallallaho alaihe wa sallam!*) demise and kissed his forehead.

Note:- This kissing was for the sake of deriving *baraka* – as the commentators of hadith have stated. But, according to Maulana Zakariya Sahib, this was a parting kiss as lasting separation was taking place from the beloved Prophet (*sallallaho alaihe wa sallam!*).

Hadith 7:- Hazrat Anas (*razi Allaho anho!*) reports that the day the Holy Prophet (*sallallaho alaihe wa sallam!*) had come to Madina, every thing of Madina had become luminous and bright and the day he passed away, every thing of Madina had become doleful and dolorous. "After his death", says Hazrtat Anas, "we had not yet shook off dust from hands when we felt change in our hearts".

Hadith 8:- It is reported from Hazrat Ayesha (*razi Allaho anha!*) that the Holy Prophet's (*sallallaho alaihe wa sallam!*) death took place on Monday.

Hadith 9:- It is reported from Hazrat Imam Baqir (*razi Allaho anho!*) that the Holy Prophet's (*sallallaho alaihe wa sallam!*) death took place on Monday. This day and Tuesday passed in making (obsequial) arrangements and he was laid to rest on the night between Tuesday and Wednesday. Sufyan, the narrator of this hadith, says that this is so as stated above in Imam Baqir's hadith, but there is also this in one narration that the sound of shovels was coming in the last part of the night.

Note:- That is, the burial ceremony took place in the last part of the night.

Hadith 10:- Hazrat Abu Salmah (*razi Allaho anho!*) reports that the Holy Prophet (*sallallaho alaihe wa sallam!*) died on Monday and was buried on Tuesday.

Note:- He was actually buried during the night between Tuesday and Wednesday, but in common parlance it is called Tuesday as well as Wednesday. Some ulema have stated that the obsequies began on Tuesday after having settled the problem of caliphate and the burial took place on Wednesday.

* * * * * * *

LXV

REGARDING THE HOLY PROPHET'S
(*Sallallaho alaihe wa sallam!*)
LEGACY

Note:- Every thing left behind by him is like sadaqah (charity). Such legacy shall not be divided among the heirs. There is consensus of the jurists over it and this is the order regarding all the prophets. There is no right of inheritance in the Holy Prophet's (*sallallaho alaihe wa sallam!*) legacy for which there are certain reasons as stated below:-

(1) The prophets are alive in their graves and hence their possession continues. It is for this reason that there is strict prohibition inn the holy Quran regarding marrying anyone of the Holy Prophet's (*sallallaho alaihe wa sallam!*) wives after his passing away.

(2) A prophet does not own anything as proper even during his lifetime, but he spends and uses it by virtue of being its manager (mutawalli).

(3) The owner of everything of this world is Allah and a prophet spends it by virtue of being His vicegerent.

(4) Had there been the order of inheritance in a prophet's legacy, it was possible that some unfortunate heir, coveting the legacy, might have become the cause of the prophet's death or might have longed for his death and thus either of these things would have become the cause of his own doom.

272

(5) The people might not suspect that the claim of prophethood had been advanced to collect wealth and bequeath it to the heirs.

(6) The prophets' holy beings had to be kept unpolluted from the corroding effect and grime of wealth.

(7) A prophet is like a father to the ummah and hence his wealth is the wealth of all the children.

Hadith 1:- Hazrat 'Amr bin Harith (*razi Allaho anho!*), who is Hazrat Juwairuyah's brother) reports that the Holy Prophet (*sallallaho alaihe wa sallam!*) had bequeathed a legacy of his weapons, his mule on which he used to ride and a plot of land - all of which he had ordered to be given away in charity.

Note:- Since included in charity, these things could not be inherited Holy Prophet's (*sallallaho alaihe wa sallam!*) clothes being ordinary have not been mentioned in this hadith.

Hadith 2:- Hazrat Abu Huraira (*razi Allaho anho!*) reports that once Hazrat Fatima (*razi Allaho anha!*) came to Hazrat Abu Bakr (*razi Allaho anho!*) and asked him: 'Who'll be your heirs"? "My wife and children", replied he. "Then", she asked, "why did I not become heir to my father's bequest"? He said: "Due to this prophetic statement that 'we do not have any inheritors'. However, I will pay the daily stipend to those people for whom the Holy Prophet (*sallallaho alaihe wa sallam!*) had fixed it and I will as well spend over those people for whom he used to spend".

273

Hadith 3:- Hazrat Ayesha (*razi Allaho anha!*) too reports the same thing that the Holy Prophet (*sallallaho alaihe wa sallam!*) said: "We have no heirs; whatever bequest we the prophets leave is sadaqah."

Note:- By 'agent' is meant the man who would become caliph or that man who collects and manages the produce of the land. The payment of the caliph's salary is a liability upon the public treasury and a superintendent or a manager too is entitled to draw his salary from it.

Hadith 5:- Hazrat Ayesha (*razi Allaho anha!*) reports that the Holy Prophet (*sallallaho alaihe wa sallam!*) bequeathed neither dinars nor dirhems, neither goats nor camels. The narrator (*ravi*) says that he has fallen in doubt whether she also mentioned "neither slave nor slave-woman" or not.

* * * * * *

274

LXVI

REGARDING SEEING
THE HOLY PROPHET'S
(Sallallaho alaihe wa sallam!)
IN DREAM

Note:- The ulema have stated that dreams are of three kinds:- (1) A dream through the angel who has been appointed for this work; such a dream is true. (2) A dream through the satanic influence. (3) A dream through one's own thoughts and apprehensions.

From a prophetic hadith, too, as recorded in the *Abu Da'ud,* it is corroborated that dreams are of three kinds: (1) The auspicious dream which is seen in the form of a glad tiding from Allah Most High. (2) The nightmare, which is engineered by Satan to terrify and afflict the dreamer. (3) The dream produced by one's own obsession and haunting fancies.

The ulema well-versed in the art of interpreting dreams have stated that the name of the angel who has been appointed to show dreams is *'Siddiqun'*.

It has been mentioned in a large number of hadiths that "whoever saw me in dream, he really saw me, for Satan has not had the power to make himself appear like me." Even so, if a man sees the Holy Prophet *(sallallaho alaihe wa sallam!)* in such a form that may not be befitting his dignity, e.g., if a man sees him in a form contrary to what has been depicted of him in the beginning of this book, it is due to the dreamer's defect

275

and not due to any flaw in the Holy Prophet's (*sallallaho alaihe wa sallam!*) personality.

Hadith 1:- Hazrat *Abd* Allah ibn Mas'ud (*razi Allaho anho!*) reports the prophetic statement that "he who saw me in dream, he saw me really, for Satan cannot make his face like mine."

Hadith 2:- A prophetic statement is reported by Hazrat Abu Huraira (*razi Allaho anho!*) also that "he who saw me in dream, he really saw me, because Satan cannot make his face like mine."

Note:- Allah Most High had saved the Holy Prophet (*sallallaho alaihe wa sallam!*) during his lifetime from the influence of Satan; similarly, after his passing away also, Allah did not invest the pantomorphic Satan with the power of making his face and features like those of the Holy Prophet's (*sallallaho alaihe wa sallam!*).

Hadith 3:- Hazrat Tariq ibn Uthaim (*razi Allaho anho!*) also reports the prophetic statement that "he who beheld me in dream, he did behold me only, because Satan cannot make his face like mine."

Note:- From these traditions arises a question as to how different people of different and distant countries have a vision of the Holy Prophet (*sallallaho alaihe wa sallam!*) simultaneously. How can he be ubiquitous - present at different places one and the same time?

The answer to this poser is that the example of The Holy Prophet (*sallallaho alaihe wa sallam!*) is like that of the sun. The sun is stationary but the people of different and distant places can see it; it need not go to all places. Similarly the Holy Prophet (*sallallaho alaihe*

276

wa sallam!) may remain where he is and yet people of different countries and distant places can see him. Moreover, if the colour of the glasses through which the sun is seen is red, green, blue or smoky, the sun too would look of the same tint. Similarly, the Holy Prophet (*sallallaho alaihe wa sallam!*) also would be seen in a form commensurate with the dreamer's psychological make-up.

Hadith 4:- Hazrat Anas (*razi Allaho anho!*) reports that the Holy Prophet (*sallallaho alaihe wa sallam!*) said: "He who saw me in dream saw me only because Satan cannot simulate me". He also said that the dream of a believer – *mumin* – (seen under the angel's influence) is one of the forty-six parts of prophethood.

Explanation:- No one can know the reality of prophethood. Similarly, the reality of the forty-sixth part of prophethood cannot be known because, says Mullah Ali Qari, it is a part of prophetic knowledge and prophetic sciences are peculiar to the prophets only and hence they alone can understand why a true dream is the forty-sixth part of prophethood. It is sufficient to know in brief that a good and auspicious dream is a good tiding and its being a part of prophethood is sufficient for its distinction, glory and *baraka*.

Imam Tirmizi has brought his book to an end with two hadiths (*athar*) which are in fact two advices and great warnings: firstly, no definite opinion should be expressed on anything through guess and conjecture; on the contrary, religion depends upon conformance to the Holy Prophet (*sallallaho alaihe wa sallam!*) and hence one should conform to him in expressing every decision. Secondly, one should not listen to every Tom, Dick and Harry but should accept the suggestion of a religious man, for an irreligious man is not worthy of conforming to. Really both these advices are very important.

(1) Abd Allah ibn Mubarak (Allah's mercy be on him!) is one of the great Imams of Hadith. He is reckoned amongst the jurists (*fuqaha*) and Sufis also and was a great Shaikh, devotee and ascetic. He says: "If you happen to become a judge (*qazi*) and adjudicator, then conform to the traditions (*manqulat*)".

Note:- That is, one should not be proud of one's own self-opinion and intelligence; on the contrary, one should adapt oneself to the statements of the great ones – the Companions – and the Hadith. This advice of Ibn Mubarak is all-inclusive, applicable to every kind of decision, whether it be the judgement of a judge or any other judgement. As stated above, Imam Tirmizi has mentioned this statement of Ibn Mubarak among the category of universal advice, as is also the opinion of the general commentators of the *Shama'il*.

Shaikh al-Hadith Maulana Zakariya Sahib, however, says that this advice is apposite to this chapter also in the sense that oneirocriticism too is a judgement of sorts and hence one should not confuse it with one's own opinion, but should study the interpretations of the predecessors. Interpretations of dreams given by the Holy Prophet (*sallallaho alaihe wa sallam!*) and the noble Companions (razi Allaho anhum!) have been copiously recorded. The experts in oneiroamancy and the art of oneirocriticism have stated that an intepreter of dreams should necessarily be an intelligent, pious and abstemious man, well-versed in the Book of Allah and the Holy Prophet (*sallallaho alaihe wa sallam!*) sunnah, and should also be aware of the Arabic parlance and language, and the widely used adages and maxims, etc.,

278

etc. Many such conditions and manners are written in the books of oneirocriticism (interpretation of dreams).

(2) Ibn Sirin (Allah's mercy be on him!) says that the science of Hadith (and all other religious sciences) are included in religion and hence it should be seen before acquiring its knowledge as to from whom it is being acquired.

Note:- Ibn Sirin too was a great Imam of his time and a distinguished Tabi'ib. He acquired different sciences from many Companions. He is also the Imam of the art of oneirocriticism and his statements regarding the interpretation of dreams are the last word. The import of his statement is that the integrity, piety, religion and tack (*maslak*) of one from whom religious knowledge is to be acquired should be thoroughly investigated, and not that one may follow any man however irreligious, he may be, for his irreligiousness will inevitably cast its evil effect. This thing has been supported in several hadiths also.

It is a general counsel but it can have relevancy with this chapter also for the science of the interpretation of dreams, too, is an important science. Since dream is a part of prophethood, however glorious its interpretation may be is obvious. It is for this reason that Imam Tirmizi has recorded this statement in the chapter on dreams. However, Ibn Sirin's statement and the contents of the hadiths are not peculiar to dreams alone but include every kind of science. Hence the greater and superior in importance a science is, the more necessary it will be to acquire it from a more knowledgeable and learned person.

In this our age, which is very near the Day of Doom, a very harmful thing, a great misfortune, that has appeared is that every man, however ignorant and irreligious he may be, pretends to be an allamah (savant) and a maulana (divine doctor) by simply wielding a lucid pen and a glib tongue, and a murshid (spiritual preceptor) and Sufi by donning a coloured dress. The masses, the common herd, due to miscomprehending the maxim that "see what is being said and not who says it", become easy victims of the fraud of such impostors. The said maxim in itself is correct but it is meant for those people who can discriminate between truth and untruth, good and evil, but those who cannot distinguish the genuine from the counterfeit, they should try to learn religion from the true scholar only.

Imam Tirmizi has ended his book with Muhammad ibn Sirin's counsel. The gist of his statement is that Hadith is religion. So first muse over it as to from whom you are acquiring your religion. The religion is established from the Holy Prophet's (*sallallaho alaihe wa sallam!*) statements and actions. Hence the hadiths should be acquired from a teacher after due thought and consideration. As long as the justness of the narrator of hadith is not proved fully, it should not be acquired from him and he should not be taken as a teacher.

The said hadith is recorded in the *Muslim* also (vol.1, p.11). It is said in *Jam'e Sagheer* that "knowledge is religion, so think as to from whom you are acquiring religion".

By knowledge (*'ilm*) is meant the knowledge of Tafsir, Hadith and Fiqh (proposition), it is reported from Imam Malik, that to acquire knowledge from an innovative or heretic (*bid'ati*) person is not permissible.

280

And knowledge should not be acquired from a person who may not have acquired it from some other (authentic or recognised) teacher. (*Mawahib*, p. 206). The reason is that the man who studies the Quran. Hadith and Fiqh without the help of a teacher, he would accept only those things from the books which would be in consonance with the desire of his self and would reject those which would be contrary to his disposition. He would make the Quran, Hadith and Fiqh subject to his desire and would go astray by omitting the propositions that would be not to his liking. The students of history know it well how many otherwise intelligent and wise men have thus deviated from the right path. It is because one having no teacher or patron tends to become a free-thinker; and hence the well-known proverb that "one who has no teacher has Satan as one's teacher".

It is stated in *Mawahib* that an innovative man should also not be taken up as a teacher because his influence would surely affect the pupil. It is for this reason that Ibn Sirin has said that Hadith is knowledge and so acquire knowledge from a teacher after knowing his antecedents and qualifications thoroughly.

The following propositions can be established from the said hadith:-

(1) A good deal of precaution is necessary in learning, teaching and writing Hadith. The Holy Prophet's (*sallallaho alaihe wa sallam!*) statement is: "Anyone who calumniates me should make his abode in Fire". (*Muslim* vol. i, p. 7).

(2) The hadiths should be narrated after due care and consideration.

(3) Investigate sufficiently about narrators of hadith to know whether an *'alim* (religious scholar) from whom hadith is to be acquired is really worthy and able or not. Accept hadith from a teacher as well as from each one of the narrators above him (i.e., preceding him) only after having considered their particulars, which ought to be in accordance with the conditions laid down by the science called *Usul-e Hadith* for the acceptance of a narration. If there be any defect or shortcoming as regards a narrator's religion, understanding, actions and memory, his narration shall be rejected.

(4) The basic knowledge consists of the Quran, Hadith and Fiqh; other sciences are subordinate to it.

(5) Effort and labour are necessary to acquire the said knowledge.

(6) By quoting the said hadith Imam Tirmizi wants to prove that he has taken pains in recording only the authentic hadiths. Since religion is established from the hadiths, one should acquire knowledge after due deliberation.

In the present times, some people, having acquired some knack of speaking and writing, have assumed themselves to be savants and are leading the masses astray. Hence it should be inquired if such a self-styled allamah has pursued knowledge in any recognised seminary or has acquired it by living in the company of an august, learned man or not; if his acquiring knowledge in the said manner is not proved, it is

282

necessary to shun him as otherwise the pupil-to-be himself will go astray.

May Allah bestow upon all the grace to act! Amen!

May Allah Most High pardon all the grave and venial sins of those gentlemen, as well as of all the young and old of their families and clans, who have rendered help and cooperation in the printing and publication of this book, and assign them an abode in the 'Illiyan and make the Holy Prophet's (*sallallaho alaihe wa sallam!*) special intercession their lot! Amen!

— AHMED EBRAHIM BEMAT

NOTES

NOTES